ART
CINCINNATI
FLYING PIG
MARATHON
POWERED BY
P&G
Walmart
50
52
RELAY
19247
17933
16045
130
12278

Flying Pig Marathon

Flying Pig Marathon

TWENTY YEARS RUNNING

CINCINNATI
20 YEARS RUNNING
FLYING PIG MARATHON®

ORANGE *frazer* PRESS
Wilmington, Ohio

ISBN 978-1939710-826

Published for Cincinnati Marathon, Inc. by:
Orange Frazer Press
P.O. Box 214
Wilmington, OH 45177
Telephone: 937.382.3196 for price and shipping information.
Website: www.orangefrazer.com

Book and cover design: Alyson Rua and Orange Frazer Press

Library of Congress Control Number: 2018943046

Printed in China

First Printing

This 20th anniversary book is dedicated to the hundreds of thousands of participants, thousands of volunteers, hundreds of medical and first responder personnel and the dozens of sponsor partners who have kept the Pig flying for twenty years. Here's to twenty more and beyond!

Contents

CINCINNATI
FLYING PIG MARATHON
INAUGURAL RUN
MAY 9, 1999

CINCINNATI
FLYING PIG MARATHON
SUNDAY
MAY 14, 2000

CINCINNATI
FLYING PIG MARATHON
SUNDAY
MAY 6, 2001

CINCINNATI
FLYING PIG MARATHON
20 SUNDAY MAY 5TH 02
AN UPLIFTING EXPERIENCE

CINCINNATI FLYING
RUN THE PIG
MAY 4 2003
SOUTHWEST OHIO AND NORTHERN KENTUCKY MARATHON
5 YEARS & RUNNING

CINCINNATI FLYING PIG MARATHON 2005

CINCINNATI
2006 FLYING PIG MARATHON

GET YOUR
Feet Revvin'

10 YEARS RUNNING
2008 CINCINNATI FLYING PIG MARATHON

FINISH SWINE
2009 FLYING PIG MARATHON

2010
0502
2010 CINCINNATI FLYING PIG MARATHON

Run the Pig
THE 2011 FLYING PIG MARATHON

PIG PARTY
FLYING PIG...A WHOLE 'NOTHER ANIMAL
2012
CINCINNATI FLYING PIG MARATHON • MAY 5-6

THE 2013 FLYING PIG MARATHON

LET YOUR IMAGINATION RUN WILD May 2-4, 2014
Pigcasso
THE 2014 CINCINNATI FLYING PIG MARATHON

We've Got
26.2 Reasons you're an
All Star
CINCINNATI · MAY 1-3, 2015
FLYING PIG MARATHON

OINKED FOR LIFE
15 YEARS RUNNING STRONG
CINCINNATI · APRIL 29-MAY 1, 2016
FLYING PIG MARATHON

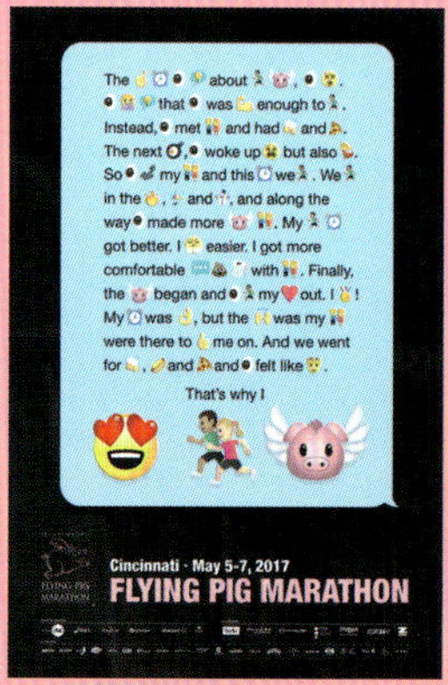
That's why I
Cincinnati · May 5-7, 2017
FLYING PIG MARATHON

CINCINNATI
IN THIS CITY WE
DREAM BIG & FLY HIGH
FLYING PIG MARATHON
MAY 4-6, 2018

Foreword

By Ryan Hall

Two-time Olympian Ryan Hall holds the U.S. record in the half marathon, finishing the distance in under an hour. He was a consultant for the Flying Pig's bid to be the host for the 2016 U.S. Olympic Marathon Trials. He ran the Flying Pig Toyota 10K in 2014 and won in an event-record time of 30:32.

I'll never forget advice my dad (he was also my coach) gave me when I was first starting out as a runner. He used to always tell me "happy feet, make light feet," meaning if you are having a good time you are going to run fast. It's so true. Looking back on it now, I can without a doubt say that the happier I was the faster I was running.

Fast forward fifteen years and I found myself on the starting stage at the Flying Pig Marathon. It was my first time attending the Flying Pig, however I had the opportunity to travel to races all over the world to make appearances. But there was something special about the Flying Pig, something different.

The first thing I noticed was the joy and humility of the staff. I felt like I was surrounded by family at the Flying Pig and that sentiment seemed to trickle all the way down to the runners. I had never attended a race where everyone seemed to be in such a good mood and so friendly towards each other.

Standing on the stage I couldn't help but smile as the thousands and thousands of runners streamed by after the starting gun fired. I couldn't contain my smile as I watched the two staff members dressed in legit pig costumes busting some serious dance moves. Those dancing pigs set the tone for the rest of the day. I felt that I was at a major race, yet I also felt that I was taking part in a celebration.

I'm so grateful that the Flying Pig began twenty years ago. It will forever be a lasting memory as I reflect back on twenty years of my own of racing and training. Here's to the past twenty years and twenty more years of happy and light feet!

CINCINNATI FLYING PIG MARATHON
2ND ANNUAL
MAY 14, 2000
3RD ANNUAL
MAY 6, 2001
4TH ANNUAL
MAY 5, 2002
5TH ANNUAL
RUN LIKE THE WIND SWEAT LIKE A PIG
MAY 4, 2003
MAY 2, 2004
7TH ANNUAL
MAY 1, 2005
8TH ANNUAL
ALL THE WAY
MAY 7, 2006
9TH ANNUAL
MAY 6, 2007
10TH ANNUAL
10 YEARS RUNNING
MAY 4, 2008
MAY 3, 2009
MAY 2, 2010
13TH ANNUAL
I MADE A RUN FOR IT!
MAY 1, 2011
14TH ANNUAL
MAY 6, 2012
THE HERO LIES IN ALL OF US
15TH ANNUAL
15 YEARS RUNNING
LET YOUR IMAGINATION RUN WILD
MAY 3 - 2015
19TH ANNUAL CINCINNATI FLYING PIG MARATHON
2017 CINCINNATI FLYING PIG MARATHON
MAY 7 2017
2018 CINCINNATI FLYING PIG MARATHON
20 YEARS RUNNING
20TH ANNUAL CINCINNATI FLYING PIG MARATHON
MAY 6, 2018 • DREAM BIG & FLY HIGH

Introduction

By Bob Coughlin

Fresh off starting his Paycor payroll processing company in 1990, Bob Coughlin, himself a runner, had the vision in 1997 to organize the board of what eventually would become the Flying Pig Marathon. Since then Coughlin has helped guide the Flying Pig through twenty years of growth and Paycor has served as a major sponsor since day one, most recently as title sponsor of the half marathon. Coughlin and his wife Jeanne provided the funding for the ArtWorks "Dream Big and Fly High" downtown mural to commemorate the Flying Pig 20th anniversary.

In May of 1999, I stood on a podium at the start of the inaugural Flying Pig Marathon in downtown Cincinnati with the mayor of Cincinnati, Roxanne Qualls. Together we shot the starting gun and watched the 6,000 participants cross the starting line. It was a nervous moment and an amazing moment to see the support and energy of the crowd.

Two years earlier, I had been working part-time to create the event, while serving full time as CEO of Paycor. I found out there was a race directors' conference in Portland the weekend of the Portland Marathon, and decided to attend along with Stacey Browning who worked with me at Paycor. Listening to the challenges and positives about other events allowed me to think about how our event could be credible, and unique.

Along the way I had been thinking about how to create an event that would attract participants to look at Cincinnati as a place to come for the weekend. We thought that the arts and culture of Cincinnati could be a differentiator, and the Flying Pig name could tie into the heritage. But to be truthful, I was not sure if the name would work.

When I returned from Portland, I was interviewed by Deb Haas, a reporter at WCPO-TV who heard about my efforts, and she made it the lead story on the news. That was rocket fuel to help get the word out. That night I got a call from Geoff Hobson, who at the time was a local sports reporter, and I mentioned the possibility of using the Flying Pig as a theme. He used it in a headline on the front page of the *Cincinnati Enquirer*, and it stuck. The rest, as they say, is history.

I set up the organization as a non-profit, and involved the local non-profit community to truly make it a community event. One key to the first year's success was that there was an 18-month buildup, giving time for the elements of the event to be developed.

The event worked because the community got behind it. One example is the Cincinnati Reds. To be credible and attract good sponsors, I wanted to get media coverage and we actively pursued *Runner's World* and the local TV and newspaper media in Cincinnati to cover the inaugural event.

Runner's World was hesitant, until the Reds offered me the ceremonial first pitch to celebrate the marathon, and we gave that opportunity to George Hirsch, the publisher of *Runner's World*. He came also because we offered him a spot on the live TV coverage. Sponsors took notice.

Cincinnati is a great community that is highlighted by the support for the event that exists today. It could not have thrived for two decades without an amazing staff, strong corporate partners, thousands of loyal volunteers and, of course, the participants who believed in us enough in those early years to take a chance on the race with a name that made them smile. I am honored and humbled to be part of the 20th anniversary celebration.

Flying Pig Marathon

May 8–9, 1999

The inaugural running of the Cincinnati Flying Pig Marathon

The inaugural Flying Pig Marathon was held on Mother's Day. The weekend featured a two-day Expo, pasta dinner, and events that included the marathon, open relay, kids' fun run and wheelchair division.

How the Flying Pig Took Flight

By Mike Boylan

Mike Boylan was the first Flying Pig Executive Director, taking a leave of absence from his law practice to serve from April 1998 until June 1999.

I was a decent high school runner, but that was about it. I was a good high school coach for a few years at Roger Bacon High School in Cincinnati, but the only distinctive skill and enthusiasm I brought to coaching, and then to road racing, was organizing and conducting events.

One thing no one locally had ever done was be a full-time director of a marathon. When the Flying Pig came to be and the organization needed its first Executive Director, I thought, I've been prepping for this position for thirty years. How hard could it be? Ha!

In April of 1998, I suddenly found myself alone in an office at 644 Linn Street, but I had several things going for me: Registration processing, banking, and later payroll were all handled without charge by Bob Coughlin's company, Paycor. Race Director Rich Williams (may he rest in peace, passed too young), had already been recruited, but would not arrive full time until November.

My first bold purchase was, with a little persuasion required for board approval, a box of 500 squeeze-toy flying pigs, with our nascent website address stamped on every little pink butt. I could not have known at the time, but those pigs brought us a break that we could only have dreamed of: Access to *Runner's World* and the ear of its staff.

Here's how it happened: Rich and I were promoting the Pig at the Chicago Marathon Expo in the basement of the Palmer House Hotel. The little squeeze-toy pigs were going way too fast, so we started an hourly raffle. When other vendors approached and asked for some pigs, I started to tell them to take a raffle number. Rich, *sotto voce,* said "Mike, that's *Runner's World*!" Whoa. So, we promised to bring some by the RW booth.

When we got to the booth after the Friday expo closing, the staff asked, "Are you going to the LaSalle Bank event?" Well, we weren't invited. "Oh, come along with us, and bring more of those pigs." We weren't on the invite list, but we bribed the check-in gals with pigs. Inside the HUGE and ornate LaSalle Bank meeting hall, we were besieged with requests for our pigs, and we were on our way.

All in all, it was a terrific experience. What I learned was—*One:* Be as generous to your sponsors and volunteers as you can with face time, praise and thanks. *Two:* An experienced mega event manager (in my case race director Rich Williams) is worth her/his weight in gold to an inaugural event. *Three:* Whenever possible, create buy-in from other charitable and civic groups, and *Four:* Create a strong board. You can't start an event like this, without a foundation like that.

Top left: Male marathon winner, Ely Rono.

Top right: Female marathon winner, Sommer Settell.

Middle left: Wheelchair male marathon winner, Saul Mendoza.

Middle right: Wheelchair female marathon winner, Deanna Sodoma.

1999

DEPAUW
479
5000
6025
1095
2265
1647
2191
5265

3311
3869
3742
2966
2497
5648
1052
6010
973
5981
1676
6755
2363
5164
1165

8142
6043

1188
1233
546
5503

200
FLYING PIG MARATHON

2145
2336
3590

718
1430
8057
1099
TEAM
6049

TEAM
1386

TO NORTH
75
3840
3226
2412
1597
1439

CENTER
WALNUT ST.
POPCORN & SWEETS

3822

May 13–14, 2000

The 2nd annual Cincinnati Flying Pig Marathon weekend

The second edition of the Flying Pig added a Corporate Relay division as well as $10,000 in prize money.

No Race Like Home

By Harvey Lewis

Harvey Lewis, a teacher at Cincinnati's acclaimed School for the Creative and Performing Arts, is an accomplished ultra-marathoner, winning the Badwater Ultramarathon and participating in Arrowhead Ultra and Marathon des Sables. He represented Team USA at the 2017 International Association of Ultrarunners 24-Hour World Championship, and won the North Coast 24-Hour National Championship Endurance Run in Cleveland. He regularly paces other runners in marathons around the world and is a Flying Pig "Streaker," completing every Flying Pig Marathon since 1999. Nearly 100 runners and walkers kept that "perfect Pig" streak alive at the 20th anniversary Flying Pig.

The Flying Pig is my favorite marathon! The Flying Pig conjures up so many memories across the years since 1999. When I ran the inaugural Pig I had no idea how much the race would grow and impact me. I had the accidental honor of somehow signing up the first year, then the second, the year after that and every year since. The race quickly became a tradition and a group known as the Streakers was born. Every first Sunday in May, I know where I will be.

It hasn't always been easy to keep the marathon streak. There was a year when college students who were my neighbors had a party and kept me up until three or four in the morning. I woke up about twenty-five minutes before the start of the race. I got ready in record time—something less than sixty seconds—had a short two-mile drive from Clifton, and ran my fastest mile of the day to the start line.

The next year I woke up with plenty of time and strolled out to my car. Two tires were flat and I decided the fastest option would be to just run to the start of the race.

In July of 2004 I broke my neck in a near fatal car wreck and had to start over with walking, but I walked back and forth to work and steadily got stronger. I began running again and the Pig came around once more, this time marking an important milestone in recovery as I strived to finish close to my previous marathon times.

One of my favorite experiences has been helping other runners reach their goals, pacing the 3:05 pace group. I've had the opportunity to pace the Pig seven times, carrying the signature signs and pink balloons. It's been so exciting to see runners finish their first marathons, reach personal records (PR) and just have fun. The team that makes up the pacers is mostly local runners, all experienced with the Pig course, and we have a great camaraderie.

The Pig is my favorite marathon because it inspires the imagination and challenges us to chase more audacious goals. I finished my first Pig in 3:19. In my twenties when I was busy with graduate school and being a young father, I slowed to four hours. Since breaking my neck in 2004, I've only gotten faster. In 2017 I ran my fastest Pig yet in 2:48, finishing 14th overall, and I hope to keep getting faster. Why not? If Pigs can fly, anything may be possible!

Now I wouldn't miss the Pig. As long as I'm alive, I'll be running the Flying Pig Marathon.

Top left: Male marathon winner, Rudolf Jun.

Top right: Female marathon winner, Rebecca Gallaher.

Middle left: Wheelchair male marathon winner, Franz Nietlispach.

Middle right: Wheelchair female marathon winner, Holly Koester.

2000

3:04:07
3:04:07
3:04:07
FLYING PIG MARATHON
FINISH SWINE
P&G
PAYCOR
Cincinnati Bell
PC on call
530-5552

Royals
#5879
S #1!!
We ♥ YOU TINE!
Go Christine
Cincinnati Bell

MEDICAL SUPPORT
MEDICAL SUPPORT
MEDICAL SUPPORT

P&G

286

FLYING
MARAT

PACERS
2881
FLYING PIG
MARATHON
5184

2217
2203

1310
445

May 5–6, 2001

3rd annual Cincinnati Flying Pig Marathon weekend

In 2001 the marathon was moved to the first Sunday in May, where it remains today.

Until the Last Pig Comes Home

By Erica Heskamp

If you have crossed the "Finish Swine" for Sunday's Flying Pig events, you've seen Erica Heskamp–although you might not recognize her in her Flying Pig mascot outfit. She has greeted runners and walkers at the finish all twenty years of the Flying Pig, no matter how hot, cold or late in the day the last finisher crosses.

In 1998, the year the marathon planning started, I called the marathon office to volunteer at a water stop. I knew from running marathons myself that water stop volunteers are essential. The person who answered the phone said they were assigning water stops to companies and non-profits and asked if I would like to volunteer to be the Pig mascot instead. Without hesitation, I said, "Sure!"

Now, I will say that when I went to the marathon office to pick up the costume two days before the very first race, I expected the Pig to look more like Scooby Doo–where you can't tell who is inside. Needless to say, I was quite shocked when I saw the pig head was on top of *my* head, and my full face was visible, let alone how big the costume was! But I was thrilled to be part of such an exciting event–and twenty years later, I'm still the Pig!

No matter what, I always stay until the last person finishes. I don't care how long it takes you–I will be there at the finish line to cheer you on and hand you your well-deserved medal. One year, at the 8+ hour mark, I saw a young man coming at me on crutches. Turns out he had fallen at Mile 20, gone to the hospital, then had the ambulance take him back to where he had fallen so he could finish. That's dedication!

The final two female finishers from 2017 also had an incredible journey together. A young woman, I believe her name was Victoria, wanted to quit and called her brother for some encouragement. Her sister-in-law, in ICU after a car crash, got on the phone and said, "If you don't quit, I won't quit." Victoria said she understood, hung up and asked God for a sign because she still wanted to quit.

Well, she got her sign. Within a few minutes, another young race participant walked up alongside her –her name was Heaven. Victoria immediately said, "That can't be true. I just asked God for a sign and he sends me someone named Heaven?" Needless to say, they finished together and Victoria asked for a second medal for her sister-in-law, who, from her hospital bed, encouraged Victoria to finish.

Being the Pig is a chance to be just a tiny part of such a large accomplishment for so many people. As each participant crosses the finish line, I give them the biggest smile I can as I look right into their eyes. The pride and joy I see is incredible. Giving them the final cheer that helps them complete their journey is what I love about the role. Whether it's your first time running the marathon or you're a Streaker, one thing you can always count on is a cheer and a smile from me as the Flying Pig as you cross the finish line. It doesn't matter if you are first or last, I will be there!

Top left: Male marathon winner, Rudolf Jun.

Top right: Female marathon winner, Rebecca Gallaher.

Middle left: Wheelchair male marathon winner, Vern Achenbach.

Middle right: Wheelchair female marathon winner, Nance Spillner.

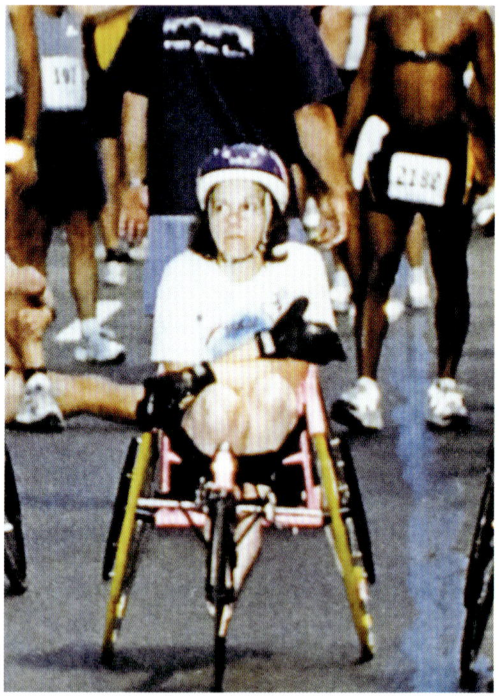

1000-2500 sf AVAILABLE
NAI EAGLE

VALET

2821

GRUNT

Go The Distance

PIG MARATHON
NISH SWINE
Cincinnati Bell
MERCY
FLYING PIG MARATHON
8212
8212
8212

JVC

PAAVO

May 4–5, 2002

4th annual Cincinnati Flying Pig Marathon weekend

In 2002 the marathon weekend added a 5-mile event on Sunday, along with $13,000 in prize money.

An Unbreakable Bond and a Precious Medal

By John Sence

Sence first made his mark running in high school, where he was on the All-Ohio team for Milford, then was a member of the All-America team in the 10,000m for Wake Forest. Among his many running accolades: He was an Olympic Marathon Trials qualifier twice, the USA National 25K Champion twice, won Cincinnati's Thanksgiving Day race and the Heart Mini Marathon seven times each, and was a 2011 inductee into Cincinnati's Running Hall of Fame. He also has served as a Flying Pig board member.

The camaraderie formed among training partners runs deep. In a sense, you prepare for battle together—pounding out miles on the streets on hot, humid summer days and cold winter months. Both of these extremes can test your desire, and you depend on your training partners to keep you going.

I had spent several years, and thousands of miles, running with Kent Enzweiler. I considered Kent a great friend—a friendship born out of our shared passion for running. He was blessed with a strong desire to compete, an incredible burn to improve and a positive, encouraging attitude that he shared with everyone.

During my "competitive" years, our training group included fifteen to twenty people, and there's no doubt that Kent was the glue of our group. I specifically remember him as the commander of our Wednesday night interval workouts at Princeton High School. These were the nights where everyone pushed themselves beyond the ordinary and where our athletic dreams were turned into reality. There is no substitute for hard work and an occasional loss of lunch on the infield!

Kent was our leader, encouraging us to lay it all on the line—even if you didn't feel like you "had it" that day. When his workout was over, Kent would stick around, encouraging, joking and reminding us to not take ourselves too seriously.

In 2001, the unthinkable happened. Kent was out for a training run when he was struck by a car. The impact tossed his body into the air like a rag doll. In an instant, he went from as fit as he had ever been to needing machines to keep him alive.

I recall the 2001 Heart Mini Marathon, where nearly everyone in the 10,000+ field wore yellow ribbons in Kent's honor. Even people who didn't know him directly rallied around him. Kent ultimately came out of his coma, but his life was forever transformed. Confined to a wheelchair, he lives with his sister, Mary, who provides the love and support he needs to carry on every day.

During the 2002 Flying Pig Marathon, Kent was still on the minds of our training group—the group Kent was part of for years. We all missed his presence and wanted to put together a relay team to compete in his honor against several city "All-Star" teams (Lexington, Louisville, Columbus and Cleveland). Our team consisted of me, TJ Lentz, Henry Dennis and Jill Tranter—all very accomplished runners and all very close to Kent.

I was fortunate to have the final 8.2 mile leg and crossed the finish line first (2:16.15)—well ahead of the second place team. I recall finishing the race, receiving my medal and immediately seeing Kent; his Dad pushing him in his wheelchair. Despite everything Kent had endured, he gave me a smile and a high five. While Kent's body had been transformed, his courage, attitude and heart had not. I proudly placed my medal around his neck and remember to this day the smile he gave in return.

For several years after the accident, Kent Enzweiler was a familiar face to Flying Pig participants, holding a prominent place on the start line platform as the honorary starter for the Flying Pig Marathon.

Top left: Male marathon winner, Cornelio Velasco.

Top center: Female marathon winner, Tatyana Pozdnyakova.

Top right: Wheelchair male marathon winner, Chad Johnson.

8791
2748
8393

WATCH FOR
EMERGENCY
VEHICLE
ONLY
ONLY
Seventh
Street
East
ONE
WAY

1776
F12
MICROHYDRIN

RELAY
GRUNT

GRUNT

2435

TEAM
7
FOR KEVIN
2407
314

2002

I N I S H S W I N E
CoActive
Marketing Group
FLYING PIG MARATHON
5151
257

5463
6425
2630
OUTBACK STEAKHOUSE
8759

CINCINNATI
1

G PIG MARATHON
NISH SWINE
paycor
MARYLYNN
7576
ANNE
TEAM
7546

Go Daddy!
CINCINNATI
FLYING PIG MARATHON

May 3–4, 2003

5th annual Cincinnati Flying Pig Marathon weekend

The 5-mile event became a 10K this year. Also added this year was a marathon 2-person relay.

First in Line for the Flying Pig

By Bob Platt

If you've participated any year at the Flying Pig, you've probably seen Bob Platt, either as a volunteer or as a participant. He was the very first person to register for the first Flying Pig Marathon, and he's still a major part of the Pig today, joining the more than 8,000 valued volunteers who give up their time over Flying Pig weekend at the Expo, on the course and at the finish "swine" to make sure events run smoothly.

My first experience with the marathon was after a run with the Leukemia and Lymphoma Society's Team in Training group, with founder Bob Coughlin and TNT coach Karen Cosgrove. Bob brought up the idea of a major marathon in Cincinnati, but I told him about the problems we'd run into as a volunteer club trying to put on races and I said it couldn't be done.

I am so glad I was wrong. Bob, his business contacts and his team put together one of the best first-time major marathons in the country. The running community across the country was in an "oink" about the race and many of them immediately added it to their bucket list as a "must do" marathon.

I was involved with the Speaker's Panel the first year, been an Expo volunteer assistant, course marshal, "Info Pig," 26th Mile volunteer, Expo vendor and just about anything else where I've been needed. I've done the marathon ten times, along with the half marathon, relay, the mile, 5K and 10K. I'm looking for a dog to borrow so I can do the Flying Fur.

There was one instance during my 150th marathon that really reminded me why I am so involved. A young lady ran up alongside me with about three miles to go. She said she knew me–but I probably didn't remember her. She explained that she ran the half marathon the year before and we had met on the bridge back to Cincinnati from Covington.

During that time on the bridge we spent a few minutes talking and she said I gave her the confidence to finish a marathon. (I'm sure the fact that I am slow and no longer have the body of a typical marathoner also helped her confidence.)

We chatted for a while, and it was obvious she was running faster than I was at the moment–I encouraged her to go on. She insisted it was her honor to run a large part of those last three miles with me. It was at that moment that I realized how a few kind words can make someone's dreams come true and anyone can be an inspiration. However, what she didn't realize is that she became one of many inspirations to me that day, along with hundreds of others, to make my 150th marathon dream come true.

Iris (Simpson Bush, the Marathon Executive Director) calls me the "number one Pig." I consider it a great honor just to have my name associated with the history of this great race, even though the only race I won was the race to the mailbox to get my entry in first, that first year.

Top left: Male marathon winner, John Aerni.

Top right: Female marathon winner, Lisa Veneziano.

Middle left: Wheelchair male marathon winner, Chad Johnson.

Middle right: Wheelchair female marathon winner, Holly Koester.

2003

8404

Turkey Bowl
St. Saviour
VS
St. John's
Classic
8514
8514
8514
8514
FLYING PIG MARATHON

FLYING PIG MARATHON
FINISH SWINE
2:59:49
2:59:49
SPARTAN CLASSIC
FLYING PIG MARATHON
1946

BOB RONCKER'S RUNNING SPOT
EAST
MILFORD, OHIO
RELAY

PIG MARATHON
ISH SWINE
CoActive
paycor
3:27·59
2563
2742
8494
8494
496

2083

504

ERNST & YOUNG
asics
8559
CINCINNATI
FLYING PIG MARATHON

2003

MARATHO
ARMY
CINCINNATI
FLYING PIG MARATHON
2791
DEACONESS

May 1–2, 2004

6th annual Cincinnati Flying Pig Marathon weekend

The Flying Pig added a walker division to Sunday's marathon this year, with an early start. A 5K also was added to Saturday's event lineup.

Bringing the World to Cincinnati

By Bob Roncker

If you are a runner in the Cincinnati area, you know the name Bob Roncker. He started coaching cross country in high school and, eventually, Xavier University but probably is best known for his chain of running stores in the greater Cincinnati area. His Bob Roncker's Running Spot training programs helped prepare thousands of runners and walkers for events each year through his store-based running groups.

I believe my first experience with the Flying Pig Marathon arrived when Bob Coughlin, the founder of the event, dropped by the Running Spot in 1997. He asked me if I thought Cincinnati was in need of a marathon. I wasn't thinking about the total community effect a marathon could bring to a place like greater Cincinnati and Northern Kentucky, so with my perceived extensive knowledge of the sport, I told Bob that I didn't think we needed a marathon. However, I mentioned that a void did exist for a half marathon event. If we were playing baseball, I'd say I was batting .500 on his question. I whiffed on the full but got it right with the half.

One of my most memorable experiences associated with the Pig was the weekend spent with the Tarahumara. In 2009, author Christopher McDougall authored *Born to Run,* which became a best seller. The story focuses on an extremely challenging race (50+ miles) within the savage terrain of the Copper Canyon (Barrancas del Cobre) region of Northern Mexico. These six coppery-tinged canyons are deeper and longer than Arizona's Grand Canyon. *Born to Run* details the race and references the Copper Canyon event as "the greatest race the world has never seen." The winner of the race that year was Arnulfo Quimare. Through an acquaintance who brought visitors to the Canyon, my wife Mary Ann and I were able to host Arnulfo, another runner, Miguel Lara, and an interpreter at our home for the 2013 Flying Pig Marathon. Since 26.2 miles was considered a short distance for them, Miguel and Arnulfo decided to run the mile event on Friday, the 10K and 5K on Saturday and the marathon on Sunday.

As it turned out, on the morning of the marathon, we were late to leave our house. We sped downtown, parked at 9th and Plum (the closest available lot) and sprinted to the start line. Fortunately, my badge as a Pig board member got us through checkpoints and we arrived at the start line with minutes to spare.

Thankfully, the marathon went well for both runners—Miguel ended up third in the Skyline Chili 4-Way Challenge (finishing all four events) and Arnulfo finished fourth! It was a delight having them at our home, giving them an opportunity to experience our city and culture and allowing other runners to meet them. A visit to Copper Canyon is definitely on my "bucket list."

Along with bringing in Miguel and Arnulfo, the Running Spot also hosted during Pig weekend Kenyan Henry Rono. In 1978 Henry set four separate track world records within the space of eighty days. Henry is arguably one of the greatest distance runners of all time. I believe that an important role of the Pig is to let the local community meet significant runners like Henry, Miguel and Arnulfo.

Top left: Male marathon winner, TJ Lentz.

Top right: Female marathon winner, PJ Ball.

THIS LIL
PIG RAN
ALL THE
WAY

PowerBar
3053

113
116

RUN
PIGGIES
RUN

1179

TEAM

FLYING PIG MARATHON
FINISH SWINE
MERCY
Health Partners
CoActive
Corporate Express
paycor
4:14·50
For Results Visit
marathon.com
4:14·50

2972
744
ML
TEAM
6203

MERCY
Health Partners
5:05·36
JAMIE
TEAM
10876
TEAM
KRISTINA
TEAM
TEAM
10503

MARGOT
10848
GINNY
Flying Pig Marathon
10526

WAY TO GO JANE
GO JANE GO!
WALK!
Go
Jane!
We love

6788
WENDY
5397

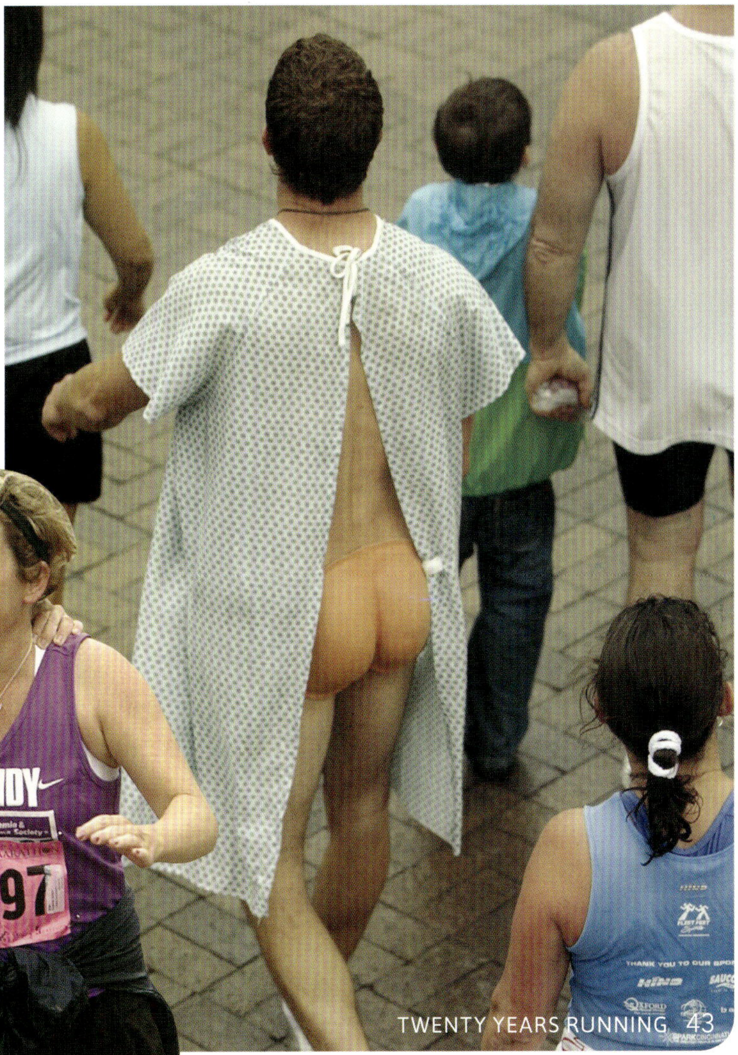

April 30–May 1, 2005

7th annual Cincinnati Flying Pig Marathon weekend

In 2005 the Flying Pig added a half marathon event and the 10K was moved to Saturday.

The Comeback Kid

By Alison Bedingfield Delgado

Alison Bedingfield was a 22-year-old soon-to-be medical student when, in 2005, she entered the Flying Pig, her first career marathon, and promptly won it. A graduate of Colerain High School in Cincinnati, where she was on the state champion cross country teams all four years, Alison faced her biggest challenge in 2010 when a traumatic head injury from a bicycle accident nearly claimed her life.

Oh, the Flying Pig Marathon, the race with the funny name! Its name is one of many things that make it special and it is a race that will always have a place in my heart.

I feel that most people who take the leap into training for a marathon are motivated by something.

When I first trained for the race in 2005, I was motivated to prove myself. After years of up and down racing performances in high school and college, I wanted to show myself and everyone else that I could train for and win a big race.

The stars were aligned on May 1, 2005; it was my day! My parents were able to follow me along the course and see me raise my hands to the sky as I crossed the line in first place. So many other loved ones were able to cheer me on from home as they watched the race on television. I had my fifteen minutes of fame for being the 22-year-old who raced and won her first marathon.

Just over five years later I faced an injury that almost took my life when I was struck by a car while riding my bike. I was blessed to have a miraculous recovery through multiple neurosurgeries and months of rehabilitation, enabling me to return to work and my normal life as a pediatrician.

I then set a new goal—to run the Flying Pig again in 2012. This time I was motivated to show that it is possible to overcome even the most horrendous obstacles. I beat my pre-injury winning time by more than two minutes. Although I did not win the race that day, it was a huge exclamation point to my comeback story: The biggest win of my life!

Tim (husband Dr. Tim Delgado) and I had actually run the Flying Pig 5K in the spring of 2011. By that point, I had returned to my residency and that race for us was kind of a celebration of what we had overcome together, getting me back to work, getting me back to running, getting me back to my normal life. I had been invited to be at the start line for the marathon the next morning in 2011 and it was then that I decided I would run the full Pig in 2012. My motivation for that marathon was to show that you can overcome even when the odds definitely seem to be against you.

Most years, a local runner wins the race: It gives the community so much pride. Most people don't get the publicity that I received, however, each runner has his or her own story. Every person who crosses that finish line is a hero. Funny name aside, Cincinnati should be proud of this race! The Flying Pig Marathon is a race where people come together, goals are achieved, and inspiration abounds. I will always love the Flying Pig Marathon!

Top left: Male marathon winner, Tim Rieger.

Top middle: Female marathon winner, Alison Bedingfield.

Top right: Wheelchair male marathon winner, Gary Forbes.

2589
292

NEWS5
WLWT-TV/DT • CINCINNATI
CINCINNATI
FLYING PIG MARATHON
Est. 1999

13549
13550
14105
15594

GO
DAD!

FLEET FEET Sports
152
HURRY ON!

National City

Philipians 4:13
3976
2120

FLYING PIG MARATHON
761
Team Stepping Stones
GAIL
1082
Team Stepping Stones
FRED
1081

Media Sponsors
BUSINESS COURIER
TIME WARNER CABLE
3887

Corporate Express
1571
3442

GO MARY
n.com

FLYING PIG MARATHON
910

May 6–7, 2006

8th annual Cincinnati Flying Pig Marathon weekend

Added events this year were the Asthma Walk and Pump 'n' Run to the 5K.

One for the Record Books

By Cecil Franke

Cecil Franke had a distinguished high school and college running career, including the 1986 Indiana High School Athletic Association 3200 meter state title at Jac-Cen-Del and school records at Ball State University. He has run Boston, run the 2007 Olympic Marathon Trials, won at Columbus and won the Flying Pig Marathon in a time of 2:20:25, an event record that has stood for more than a decade. He now teaches and coaches at Centerville High School in Indiana.

In 2006, I had the privilege of running the Flying Pig Marathon at thirty-eight years old. It was only the second marathon in my career, but the events of the day and the hospitality of the city and organization made it extremely memorable.

Having run the Columbus Marathon, Boston and the Olympic Trials, I can say that no other marathon has as many water stations and fantastic volunteers. The course was well-lined with spectators and workers to keep traffic from interfering with a great race as well as great directions to help keep the runners on the course.

The race starts early, which helps the chances of perfect temperatures and great scenery as the morning sun catches the course. Crossing the bridges and heading toward Eden Park, especially between Miles 5 and 9, makes you glad that you came prepared.

As you cover the 26.2 miles, you will see everything from live bands to volunteers dressed like pigs. The helicopter flies overhead, making for great television coverage of the race as commentators back at the finish area keep the television audience aware of what's happening with the leaders as well as unique participants.

Having been fortunate to set the event record for the marathon course, I think the Flying Pig Marathon will always have a special place in the memories of my running career. I cannot state enough how hospitable the city and the race organizers were and how well I was treated after the race.

It also holds a special place with me because it raises money for worthy causes and is not just a money-making venture like some other races. If you are trying to decide where to do your next spring marathon, I would highly recommend the Flying Pig as it is a great race executed by great people.

Top left: Male marathon winner, Cecil Franke.

Top center: Female marathon winner, Norah Shire.

Top right: Wheelchair male marathon winner, Mark Graham.

2006

14618
14594
15595

Gold
Sponsors
16968

3145

CINCINNATI
9379
CINCINNATI
9379

WE
LOVE U
ANGELA
WE LOVE
YOU,
ANG!

www.Team413.org
I can do all things through Christ who strengthens me.
Philippians 4:13

SWIN
CLIFPACE

I'm an Englishman in Cincinnati
4074

1695

2006

2819

6:00

GIRLS
RUNNING
MARATHON

TORPEDOES

CLIF PACE
Marathon #1
Wish Me Luck
CLIF

May 5–6, 2007

9th annual Cincinnati Flying Pig Marathon weekend

Added this year was the Hope and Possibility event for physically challenged participants. The Flying Piglet incremental marathon was expanded with a "Hog Log" to track miles.

Thank You, Thank You Very Much

By Jim Jones

As Flying Pig participants make their way through Eden Park, they've been greeted for more than a decade by the golden tones of "The King." Jim Jones' Elvis tribute is one of the most popular entertainment spots along the course, chosen as one of the top three entertainment zones nearly every year. "Elvis" is one of more than 100 musical acts, cheer squads and fun zones scattered along the half and full marathon courses that keep participants motivated as they head toward the "Finish Swine."

I remember my first Flying Pig. I had been performing as "Elvis" for only two years, and I had never done anything like this. I arrived at Krohn Conservatory in Eden Park really early. It was still dark. I was set up and ready to go with at least an hour to spare.

Then they started to come. The first runners were the serious ones. Then gradually, the runners began to high five me. Some even sang along. There were thousands of them, and they seemed to enjoy my performance as much as I enjoyed singing.

As the years have gone by, many runners have their phones with them and stop to take a picture with me. This still amazes me! One guy takes a picture every year. We strike the same pose each year. He said he has them on a wall in his basement. The latest thing seems to be group pictures. That's always a blast! The guy dressed as the "Shark" running by each year makes me smile. We always high five. I don't think we've done a picture.

Last year a group of runners stopped and all handed their phones to a man who was there to take pictures. About four pictures in, he realized he was using the wrong phones for some of them! Some people retook, others went on. My daughter Stephanie was with me one year and when people saw other runners hand her phones for pictures, they stopped, too. She had to have them line up.

I'm happy that so many have told me that hearing me gets them up the hill there. Throughout the year I'm always asked if I'm the Flying Pig Elvis. I proudly answer, "Yep." I'm amazed that so many runners stop to thank me for being there.

The 20th anniversary of the Pig is my 18th in a row. I'm not sure if anyone has performed longer at consecutive Pigs. I can't describe how much fun I have during the event. The smiles on peoples' faces as they run, or in some cases walk by, bring me joy. The last runners are so appreciative that I stay until the end. And so many people are helped by the charities! Again, a source of pride for me.

How long will I continue with the Flying Pig? As long as they let me get away with it. Thanks for allowing me each year to perform and, in some small way, help out.

Here's to many more Pigs!

Top left: Male marathon winner, Isaac Barnes.

Top center: Female marathon winner, Leah Peelman.

Top right: Wheelchair male marathon winner, Mike Savicki.

NO
PARKING
ANY
TIME

FLEET
FEET
1325

FULL
MARATHON

SIDEWALK
CLOSED

GRUNT
FOR GLORY
ENDURANCE

ONLY
ROAD
CLOSE

3:40·04
2043

3:52:24
Duke Energy
Let's Get Active
Let's Get Active
FLYING PIG MARATHON
277

4:19:37
3832

1425
2487

10785
National City
10045
National City

FINISH SWINE
National City
9521

FINISH SWINE
National City
FLEET FEET

7:54:38

CINCINNATI POLICE

GRUNT
rst
Aid

May 3–4, 2008

10th annual Cincinnati Flying Pig Marathon weekend

The Flying Pig's 10th anniversary was celebrated with 165 Streakers. Chip timing was added for the 5K, and the Flying Pig began a new partnership with the Cincinnati Reds for Pig Night at the Ball Park, honoring Flying Pig finishers with pre-game ceremonies.

An Unplanned New Route

By Scott Krauser

On May 4, 2008, the Flying Pig was celebrating its last day of its 10th anniversary running with a record crowd when an early morning fire along Mile 22 of the course forced last-minute changes and created a marathon to remember. Police Specialist Scott Krauser was the Cincinnati police officer in charge of the safety and security of the marathon course.

I would begin my patrol of the marathon route every year at 1 a.m. and continue until the start of the race to make sure the course was safe. We would watch for incidents in the early morning hours, from DUIs along the setup area to aggressive animals in the park, but this year would be like no other.

While we were getting the course ready for the run by pre-placing traffic control pieces (traffic cones, barricades, etc.), I found out there was a house fire on Eastern Avenue. I immediately radioed to my direct supervisor, Sgt. Greg Lewton, told him I was on my way to check out the situation and would keep him apprised. When I got there, I immediately saw the marathon was in jeopardy based on the size of the fire, the amount of equipment that was in the street, and the time of morning.

Since the entire marathon route has to be clear before the first runners can take off, we were looking at up to a four-hour delay before we could start. We knew it would be hard to ask runners to go off routine and stick around for a later start time, so I began to run scenarios through my head as to how we could continue to maintain the same route.

With thousands of runners already heading to the start line downtown and the marathon set to go off at 6:30 a.m., the clock was ticking for us to figure out what to do to make sure the event could still take place on time. I pulled maps that I had created for each zone of the course that showed me other connecting streets and that helped us start planning out other routes. Once I found the streets that connected, I called Sgt. Lewton to tell him we had the possibility of making the route change, but it would take a little work and a lot of cooperation.

The new route was going to use the city street as well as a bicycle trail, then a driveway and back onto a city street. The Cincinnati Recreation Commission controlled the driveway and the bicycle trail. I found their service building and was able to find a worker (that early in the morning!!). He drove with me, we were able to open gates, and he began to clear the bicycle path of any debris. I began reconfiguring my traffic officers to protect the marathon as it came through this area and figured out our volunteer needs to help direct runners and walkers along the detour.

We were about an hour away from the marathon's scheduled start when Sgt. Lewton and Flying Pig Executive Director Iris Simpson Bush headed out to see the house fire firsthand. By the time they had arrived, we had the plan and I just needed approval from them to continue. They were able to view the new portion of the route to decide if it would work or not. They gave the detour the green light, and the marathon was delayed by only a few minutes instead of the hours it would have taken to clear the fire scene.

Without the cooperation of city officials, park employees and volunteers, we would have never been able to adjust to the emergency and ensure a safe course for the participants. It added about a quarter mile to the marathon, but runners took it in stride (pun intended) and the Boston Marathon even accepted the adjusted times of those who qualified. Sometimes you get lucky and everything just falls in place to help solve a major problem. This was one of those situations.

Marathon Executive Director Iris Simpson Bush has her own observations about that morning:

On race morning, I usually arrive about 3 a.m. just to check out last minute set up and actually, it is usually very organized and methodical, so it's my "calm before the storm." Some runners begin arriving between 4:30 and 5 a.m., so I don't have the opportunity (or need) to drive the entire course. I do often drive Riverside Drive and Eastern Avenue since it is at the end of the course and its proximity just gives me a perspective and comfort level for the day.

On the infamous fire morning Scott has described, I had just driven Riverside and was coming by Adams Landing when a Fire Marshal went speeding by—my thought was "that doesn't look good!" I continued on to the finish and within two minutes, I got a call saying there was a fire on the course.

As I pulled into the finish, I jumped into the police car with Don Connolly, our race director at the time, and Sgt. Greg Lewton who has been with the Pig since year one. We raced to the fire location and the Fire Marshal told us that there would be at least a four-hour delay. My heart fell, because as anyone who has ever planned a marathon knows, that's just not possible.

As he is telling us that, Officer Krauser pulls up and gets out of his cruiser—in full uniform with clipboard in hand! I was amazed because even though he was always integrally involved in course planning, he was on paternity leave. His wife had just delivered their second child four days before and we had already been advised that he couldn't be available on race morning.

Not only had he come to work of his own volition, he literally saved the day. He had already worked out a detour that would have minimal impact on the neighbors (who already had to deal with the effects of a dangerous fire). He then proceeded to oversee race operations at the fire site while we returned to the start. Because of an excellent communication chain and with assistance from local media, we were able to advise everyone involved of the delay and the race start was indeed only fifteen minutes late.

So, although Scott's perspective of the fire year is factual and accurate, there is much more to the story. He truly was our hero! He went way beyond the call of duty and amazed everyone with his quick and effective response. Running publications across the country picked up the story and several referred to it as a textbook example of how to handle an emergency.

I have felt extremely fortunate to have the city support and vested relationship with our special events unit. This was proof positive that it takes an entire community to build the kind of event the Flying Pig Marathon has become. Now you know "the rest of the story!"

Left: Male marathon winner, Andy Martin.

Right: Female marathon winner, Michelle Didion.

2008

2319
3108

ROAD CONSTRUCTION AHEAD
HALF MARATHON

10 YEARS RUNNING

RUNNER'S
LOUNGE
FREE BEER

10 YEARS RUNNING
grunt
ENTERTAINMENT
2008

2816
ARMY

CANADA
2722
2896

PATRICK CONREY'S
RUN FOR HEROES
9364
6510

2221

DAN
5010
SELIMA
4329
3847
972

CINCINNATI
FLYING PIG MARATHON
TOYOTA
START
TOYOTA FLYING PIG 10K
TOYOTA
CINCINNATI
FLYING PIG MARATHON

12588
18069

I WILL, we WILL...
In remembrance
9082
9144

May 2–3, 2009

11th annual Cincinnati Flying Pig Marathon weekend

In 2009, the Flying Pig kicked off the first year of a recycling/reuse effort called the "Greening of the Pig." Also added on Saturday was the Family Fun Festival during kids' events.

The Beginning of a Marathon Habit

By Marty and Denise Hovey

Marty Hovey is not only a Streaker, he is on his way to running a marathon in all 50 states. He and his wife, Denise, have been involved with the Flying Pig since the beginning. Denise was a long-time staff member at the Flying Pig and now coordinates the greening program for all Pig-related events.

Marty: My first experience with the Flying Pig Marathon was the inaugural event in 1999. My wife Denise saw an ad in the local newspaper asking for volunteers to work on the marathon. She wanted to be involved but was not a runner, so she volunteered in registration. She suggested I run the marathon, since I had run 5K and 10K races. At first, I hesitated but found a training program and began to prepare. I ran the inaugural Flying Pig Marathon and it was the first of my now sixty-six marathons.

I have been involved with the Pig since the beginning for a few reasons. Since Denise was involved, I had a special connection with the staff. Over the years, I have enjoyed the events, the people and the training involved with the Flying Pig Marathon. I have made many new friends, some who have traveled with me to out-of-state marathons.

I heard about the 50 States Club and began to think about completing a marathon in every state, and in 2008, I became a coach at Fleet Feet Sports to help others get to the "Finish Swine." Looking forward to even more friends and runners joining us for the Flying Pig!

Denise: What started in 2009 as a simple plan of three volunteers collecting plastic water bottles at the finish line has grown to a nationally-recognized program of sustainability in sports. Working with the Council for Responsible Sport, the Flying Pig Marathon has expanded its sustainability efforts beyond Resource Management to also include Access and Equity, Community Legacy, Procurement, and Planning and Communication. These pillars of sustainability guided us in establishing our goals to reduce our environmental footprint, continue to reach out to athletes of all abilities, and to share our knowledge of sustainability with the public.

Each year since 2009, when we collected nearly a ton of plastic to be recycled, our sustainability program has grown to not only recycling 5.45 tons of plastic and cardboard, but also recycling and donating another 4.65 tons of recyclable items in 2017, resulting in 78% of waste diverted from the landfill.

The Flying Pig has been recognized for its efforts by being awarded the 2011 Excellence in Public Recycling, 2015 Green Business Award for Green Practices, 2015 certification as a green event at the Gold level, and the 2017 Gold Level Inspire Certification. All of this could not have been accomplished without the more than 300 Green Team volunteers, Green Venue Managers, and the Flying Pig staff.

Left: Male marathon winner, Sergio Reyes.

Right: Female marathon winner, Autumn Ray.

HALF
HALF
FULL
FULL

CINCINNATI FLYING PIG MARATHON
GRUNT
2009 FLYING PIG MARATHON

asics
AGGIES

ENTER
TURPIN

LORD'S
RUN

FINISH
15281
12123

Boston
Marathon
3577

11837

3:27:47
UNIVERSITY OF
KENTUCKY
northern
rock

May 1–2, 2010

12th annual Cincinnati Flying Pig Marathon weekend powered by P&G

P&G took over title sponsorship of the Health & Fitness Expo, and this was the final year the Flying Pig printed a promotional brochure. After this year, materials would be posted on line to save resources.

It's Never Too Late

By Mike Fremont

When you think you're too tired to get out and run, or think that being in a marathon is for younger folks, think of Mike Fremont. He was 96 years young for the 20th running of the Flying Pig Marathon. Running was a passion that came to him late in life, but Mike proves every day that age is just a number.

As a Streaker (I own a Flying Pig commemorative jacket that says so) I always thought a Streaker was a guy who had too many beers dashing nude through a mixed campus and the town. And getting arrested. Now that I am a Streaker I am proud to carry the title—and wear the jacket.

Anyway, what we had locally before the 1999 inaugural Flying Pig Marathon was the Covington YMCA race out past Ludlow's sewage treatment plant (which may, by that time, have become a fish farm!) and up a terrible hill to start *and* finish, and the Mt. Airy race.

At Mt. Airy's maze of trails my wife borrowed a bike and met me at many corners. She was wearing blue jeans, I remember, and at one of our meetings she yelled, "Guess what? I blew a tire!" I replied, "I know, you're wearing blue attire!" So the Pig alternative was really a boon to us runners.

The last time I ran Boston was in 2005 at age 83. It was 85 degrees at the start with a gentle, flowing breeze and stayed that way the whole race. It took 20 minutes to get to the starting line from Corral 21 (of 22 total; 1,000 runners each).

Some of my Flying Pig memories: Running the Pig in 2004 at Mile 24, I encountered Karen Doppes Cosgrove, who offered me a salt packet. I said to her, "Karen, I'm 10 minutes slower than last year," and she said, "But Mike, you're not 82 anymore!"

In 2010, I ran the Pig at age 88 and set a world single-age record (look up World Single Age Records-Marathon) and two U.S. records before that, and ran Huntington's Marshall University Marathon in 2012 and set the world record for age 90. Then I ran at Morrow, Ohio, and set a world half marathon record for age 90, then ran Knoxville's half marathon and set a world record for the half at age 91. So I'm a world record holder but too slow for Boston!

I am absolutely certain that the reason I can run long distances at my age is my whole foods, plant-based diet, begun at age 70. My advice for those who wonder if they're too old for running? Be patient. Give yourself a chance. Running in old age has been amazing and wonderful for me, beyond my capability to describe.

Left: Male marathon winner, Brian List.

Right: Female marathon winner, Cynthia Arnold.

1410

GRUNT

FINISH SWINE
P&G
1:56-22
1:56-22

Earth Drummers
4293

Love God
Love People

teamP&G
8088

Elm Street
PUT YOUR BIG GIRL PANTIES ON & DEAL WITH IT

CINCINNATI
FLYING PIG
MARATH
Thanks to the Greater Cincinnati
Police Depts.
Fire Depts.
Medica Professionals
"Our Heroes!"
FLYING PIG MARATHON
Burke

FLYING PIG
MARATHON
asics
3685

NE
MKTG

FINIS SWINE
2010 FLYING PIG HALF MARATHON

P&G

April 30–May 1, 2011

13th annual Cincinnati Flying Pig Marathon weekend powered by P&G

The Flying Pig increased its charity component this year with the Piggest Raffle Ever in partnership with CancerFree Kids. The Pig also added a fall event, the Who Dey 5K, partnering with the Marvin Lewis Community Fund. The Pig also was certified as a Green Event by the Council for Responsible Sport.

Community Partners Power the Pig

By Frances Gilbert

Frances Gilbert has been a member of the Flying Pig Marathon board for twenty years and served two years as recording secretary. She travels the country with members of the Avondale Running Club to participate in marathons and half marathons, and helps with volunteer coordination each year at the Pig.

My first experience with the Flying Pig Marathon was a request to serve on the board of directors. A running friend approached me and asked me if I would like to be part of the marathon and represent the running community. I agreed and joined the board shortly thereafter.

We're proud that the Flying Pig continues to grow after twenty years. I think the Pig's administration staff and its respect for people behind the scenes is responsible for the marathon's longevity to date. The Flying Pig Marathon is involved with other community events and charities and that's a big part of what has made me want to continue my involvement. It gives back to the community and it protects and gives back to the environment through recycling, neighborhood clean ups and a general passion for doing the right thing.

The give back to the community has made this event an icon. The economic impact, the way it showcases the neighborhoods and local attractions, the way it raises money for so many charities and the way it represents my home town makes me proud and honored to be a part of it all.

I continue to do this because I enjoy being a part of such a big and successful event. Getting to work the finish line and witness the enthusiasm and sense of personal accomplishment so many experience as they finish always sticks with me.

I'm especially moved by the commitment, passion and dedication of our Streakers—those who have run all twenty Flying Pigs! The fact that they plan their lives, their training and all that it takes to be here and finish every year is an inspiration.

I'm one of the founding members of the Avondale Running Club. When I began my involvement with the Flying Pig I thought it would be a good association and was able to bring the club in as a community volunteer group.

The Avondale Running Club has been involved all these many years and both organizations have benefited greatly. I'm proud to have been able to be a part of both and the good work they do. It warms my heart that both groups are flourishing in our community.

Left: Male marathon winner, Kieran O'Connor.

Right: Female marathon winner, Amy McDonaugh.

2011

MEDICAL
MEDICAL

RUN FASTER...
MY ARMS ARE GETTING
TIRED !!!
RUN ABBY RUN!
WE'RE PROUD OF YOU!

RIO IN DIGITAL 3D
JANE EYRE
THE DUEL
MARIEMONT

2011 FLYING PIG HALF MARATHON
FLYING PIG HALF MARATHON
Erica
17855
Robillard
21540

がんばれっ

7785

STITES
Flying Pig

May 5–6, 2012

14th annual Cincinnati Flying Pig Marathon weekend powered by P&G

To recognize long-time participants, the Flying Pig in 2012 added the Squadron designation, to honor those who had completed five or ten Flying Pigs. The Squadron was later expanded to include fifteen years.

Divine Intervention

By Mary Enzweiler

A marathon runner herself, Mary Enzweiler has been involved with the Flying Pig since the beginning as a board member, volunteer co-ordinator and now the self-proclaimed "minister of fun." When you see the "Twist and Snout" or "Hog Wash" stations, those are all the creations from Mary's 'piggy' imagination. But it doesn't happen without the generosity of those along the course and more than 8,000 volunteers.

The Flying Pig Marathon—always the first Sunday in May. Sounds like a great day for a marathon. Well, yes, if one is running. Maybe not so wonderful for a church trying to conduct Sunday morning services. One of the unique attractions of a marathon is that it offers the participants a foot tour of the city via traffic-free streets.

Organizers of the Pig realize that the marathon and half-marathon routes affect the most important day of the week for the area's churches and appreciate the understanding, cooperation, and participation of those impacted. The Flying Pig has become a uniting community event and churches have contributed in a variety of manners to that community appeal.

Runners approaching the Mile 14 water stop are served by Nativity Parish from Pleasant Ridge, just as they have since the beginning, along with Grace United Methodist, and St. Jude. These three organizations were volunteering at the Pig in year one and for many years thereafter handing out water and Gatorade to thirsty marathoners.

Any runner assigned to the final leg of a relay team has experienced the kindness and hospitality of Linwood Baptist Church on Eastern Avenue. Linwood Baptist generously moves its morning service to the evening and opens its facility to the Pig. How about those fresh, cool, refreshing, peeled orange slices, runners? Thank the Linwood Baptist volunteers! Spectators have also experienced the generosity of Union Baptist Church on Seventh Street. Union Baptist allowed the Spectator Party Zone visitors to enjoy a rare pleasure in downtown Cincinnati—a nice green grassy area.

Not from the area? No problem. The Pig welcomes churches from far and wide. For a couple of years, marathoners were treated to an almost surreal experience on Eastern Avenue (now Riverside Drive). The singers from Crossroads Christian Church in Newburgh, Indiana, traveled more than 200 miles to provide a chorus that elicited emotional chills to the runners.

Although the heart and soul of any church is its people, the actual edifice of St. Francis de Sales in East Walnut Hills plays a key role with the Flying Pig. It is where, as the runners approach the church, they must make the decision to go right or left because at this point the full and half marathon courses split. Decisions have consequences.

To say the Flying Pig has been blessed to have these and many, many other religious organizations as part of the event is an understatement. A sincere 'thank you' hopefully means so much.

Left: Male marathon winner, Sergio Reyes.

Right: Female marathon winner, Rachel Bea.

2012

12923
1336

2012
FLYING PIG
#1827 Lets Go Nikki!
2012

CINCINNATI PARROTHEAD CLUB
VOTE
MILE 18

CANCER
SUCKS
FLYING PIG
8426

Boston (Marathon) Strong

By Dave McGillivray

The 2013 Boston Marathon bombing happened less than two weeks before the Flying Pig events. Pig organizers didn't know if the bombing would scare people away from participating. Instead, the opposite happened. Many Flying Pig events reached capacity at the Expo because of a last-minute rush of registrations. Flying Pig participants donated to the One Fund Boston, wrote notes of support at the Expo and purchased #BostonStrong shirts and bracelets, with proceeds going to the bombing victims.

Dave McGillivray, the race director for the B.A.A. Boston Marathon, has been a friend of the Flying Pig for many years. Here are his reflections of that day in April.

I used to always think, "it's *only* a road race." Then in 2007 came a Nor'easter. And in 2012 it was the oppressive heat. And then the bombings in 2013. I've now changed my stance–it definitely is much more than a road race.

The conditions on the morning of April 15, 2013, could not have been better. Everything, and I mean everything, was going perfectly that morning. Although a bit chilly early in the morning, it was a sign that it would be ideal running conditions. A check with our public safety officials at 8 a.m. indicated all systems go, no issues.

At 8:52 a.m. we conducted a "moment of silence" for the victims of the tragedy in Newtown, Connecticut. It was riveting. You could hear a pin drop in the entire town of Hopkinton. Little did we know then that seven hours later we would be experiencing our own tragedy.

All the divisional starts went off on time. As I usually do, I rode on a lead motorcycle in front of the elite men. Once again, everything along the course was nailed. The crowds were huge with no signs of things to come.

At approximately 12:09 p.m., I arrived at the finish and watched the men's winner cross the finish line. Then I saw my family seated in the bleachers, went over to them, hugged them and took a peaceful family photo with them. Tom Grilk, Executive Director of the B.A.A. (Boston Athletic Association) and race announcer leaned over and asked me how I thought things were going. I answered to the crowd in the bleachers, "flawless, wonderful, a beautiful day."

At 1:30 p.m., I texted Grilk and said I've checked with everyone and everything was going well and would it be okay to now head back out to Hopkinton to begin my run of the course as I have done for the last twenty-five years. His response was comforting–"beat it"–meaning, he, too, felt all was on automatic pilot. We have the best, most experienced team on the planet. Everyone was in good hands but if needed, I was only a phone call away.

We arrived back in Hopkinton at 2:48 p.m. At 2:52 p.m., the "call" came–there had been a bombing at the finish. Shock and disbelief were my immediate reactions. Then nervousness about the safety of my own family who was still sitting in the stands. I called my wife, Katie, to see if she and our children were okay. I could not immediately get through to her.

The decision to head back to Boston right away was a no-brainer. There were two Massachusetts State Police motorcycle troopers waiting for us at the start line. We asked if they would escort us to the finish, not going down the course like they had intended but heading back out to the Massachusetts Turnpike. We went more than 100 miles an hour down the Pike and got back to Boston in twenty minutes at about 3:19 p.m.

I couldn't believe my eyes when we arrived at the corner of Clarendon and Boylston streets. It was as if the bombs went off throughout the entire post finish line area with supplies and equipment spewed all over the streets. We were fortunate we had a State Police escort because even with our credentials, I am not sure we would have been let back into the secured area.

I immediately jumped out of the car and headed for the medical tent. My heart sank seeing some of the innocent victims of the bombing, but I also knew that they were in good hands with our medical crew.

I wanted to head to the finish line itself but the police already had that secured off—even my Race Director ID could not get me into the secured area. That's when I really knew a lot of this was out of our hands and all being handled by public safety officials. It was a strange feeling not being able to go where I wanted to go in my own race. My attention then focused on our runners and doing what we could to help them be safe, retrieve their gear and reunite with their family and friends.

By nightfall, all the runners were taken care of so we reconvened as a staff in the hotel until approximately one o'clock in the morning.

For me, the two weeks following the blast consisted of helping to clean up Boylston Street while dressed in a hazmat suit, attending the wake of one of the victims who was from Medford, Mass., where I grew up, a brief meeting with President Obama during his visit to Boston, answering more than 3,000 emails and text messages from kind and caring people from all over the country and the world, dealing with the overwhelming amount of media interest and completing my own run of the course quietly and respectfully eleven days later.

The amount of support and love that continues to be expressed to all of us has been amazing. No act of terror will deter or dampen the great spirit of the endurance community. We still give thanks to all the first responders and volunteers who ran toward the explosions and not away from them, saving so many who may not have survived if not for their bravery and courage. If there is a positive to consider, it is the fact that the bombings occurred within yards of hundreds of the best medical professionals in the world.

With the amazing support of the entire running community, we all have persevered, we have recovered, but we will never forget those who were profoundly impacted. The 2014 race the following year was EPIC. We are in solidarity with each other and we are back stronger than ever.

Left: Male marathon winner, Sergio Reyes.

Right: Female marathon winner, Rebecca Walter.

BOSTON
STRONG
FLYING PIG
MARATHON
P&G
asics
Ms. Betsy:0)
2067
CORRAL
H

GRUNT
GRUNT

BOSTON RUNNER STOPPED AT 25.2
FLYING PIG MARATHON

I LIKE PIG BUTTS
AND I CANNOT LIE
20446
2657
2656
15328
20973
47296

DON'T
WEAR
OUT
.com

2013
PIGLET START
Pampers
FirstWatch
BIG BOY

YOU'RE AMAZING
RUN 4 BOSTON

WALNUT HILLS
8
EAGLES

May 2–4, 2014

16th annual Cincinnati Flying Pig Marathon weekend powered by P&G

The Flying Pig prides itself on having an event for everyone, so this year the Flying Fur Run was added for dogs (including their own finisher's medal).

Running for a Cause

By Karen Cosgrove

Karen Cosgrove is one of the original planners of the Flying Pig Marathon and has trained thousands to run marathons for charity, first with Team in Training for the Leukemia-Lymphoma Society, and most recently for Miles That Matter. She also qualified and ran in the 1984 and 1988 Olympic Marathon Trials. The winner of the inaugural Columbus Marathon, Cosgrove has run more than 110 marathons in her career—her 100th was the Flying Pig Marathon in 2008.

I can't believe it has been twenty years! It feels like it was just yesterday that I was in Portland, Oregon, running a marathon with Bob Coughlin. We were attending the race director's conference and I was there with Bob to learn if it would be possible to host a major marathon in our city. There were a few naysayers back home and I needed to be convinced that it could be done. A marathon in Cincinnati—WHEN PIGS FLY!

It was on Tuesday following the trip to Portland that I found myself in a bar across the street from the Running Spot (with Bob Coughlin), drawing a map of the potential race course on a napkin from that bar. With map in hand, I met Bob the following Sunday morning early and we drove that potential marathon course. Yes, it all started with a bar napkin, and the rest is history. The saying is so true, "Time flies when you're having fun."

Crossing the finish line of the very first Flying Pig Marathon (with tears in my eyes) was surreal for me. It was like running my first Olympic Marathon Trials all over again. It was an amazing experience and one I will never forget! I knew that day I was so blessed to have a marathon like the Pig in my own back yard. I knew we had a winner and something big in our pockets. Going from 6,000 to nearly 40,000 in twenty years is pretty impressive. I often wonder what the naysayers think today.

I have traveled the world, run lots of marathons and people ask me all the time, "What is your favorite marathon?" I reply without hesitation, "Cincinnati Flying Pig Marathon." Nothing compares to the Flying Pig! It's the best sporting event our city has to offer. There is something for everyone. For me, it has become a "Pay It Forward" marathon. I have been able to coach thousands of everyday athletes to finish their marathons, and I've been able to remind and help those athletes give back to people in need. Promoting fitness and good will in our community is so important to me.

So each year on the first Sunday in May, I come back to the Pig for many reasons. I come back to be reminded of the generosity and compassion in our community. I experience firsthand people running or walking, volunteering, cheering and showing their love for one another. I come back to see the excitement and happiness on so many faces. I come back to get my fill of sweaty embraces at the finish line. I love the Pig and all it represents. It makes me proud!

Left: Male marathon winner, Sergio Reyes.

Right: Female marathon winner, Amy Robillard.

2014

START

HORSESHOE
CASINO
THE 2014 CINCINNATI FLYING PIG MARATHON

BLISTERS
HURRY UP! THE HALF-MARATHONERS ARE EATING ALL THE FOOD!
LOVELAND

Buckeye
FLYING PIG MARATHON
4670
4378
4374

AGGIES
4750

Free Hugs

1 GREENE
2 GREENE
RED GREENE
BLUE GREENE
GO! GO! GO!
KEEP ON GOING
JANINE PLEASANT,
MICHELLE LEE,
JILL HAYTER, &
MELISSA CLEMENS!!!
Go Brandy Cole!
Brandy runs dandy!
Don't quit when you're tired
Quit when you're DONE
RUN RACHEL RUN!
Go Debbie
Suck it up Princess!
Isaiah 40:31
go Victoria Sabato!
you got this,
the finish line
GO Nonna!
LISA SCHNEIDER -
WE LOVE YOU
MOMMY!!!
GREAT JOB
ERIC, GREG, BRAD
JENNIE, JANAYE,
DAWN & MADISON!
Run, Lisa, Run!

FREE
HIGH 5
GUY!

CINCINNATI
PARROT
HEAD
CLUB
VOTE
MILE 18
FLUID STATION

2186

May 1–3, 2015

17th annual Cincinnati Flying Pig Marathon weekend powered by P&G

The Flying Pig introduced a new app with information on registration, course maps and more. The event also was recertified as a Green Event by the Council for Responsible Sport at the Gold Level.

A Mom First, A Runner Second

By Amy Robillard

Amy Robillard has won every Flying Pig event she has entered, from the half marathon to the full. She represented the Cincinnati area at the 2016 Olympic Marathon Trials in Los Angeles.

Getting through the year of 2010 was nothing short of a miracle, so to have signed up for the Flying Pig Half Marathon in 2011 was surreal. I had zero expectations and I was consumed with what was happening at home with my two kids, one of whom was only eight months out from a bone marrow transplant.

The pace of normalcy was resuming for my family, but I treaded lightly heading to the start line, and as soon as the gun went off I just ran and my mind went numb. I cannot recall the depth of my emotions, but I knew I felt more like myself than I had in years, and I have never smiled so much after a race.

I ran hard, finished it, met some amazing people and bolted home. I do remember walking in the door before 9 a.m. to attend to my son's needs, not really grasping that I had won and ran in a time that would have made me laugh hours prior. The Flying Pig experience made me want to run again the following year, if all was going well for my son.

Thankfully, I was able to race the half marathon again in 2012. A more stable home life gave me the opportunity to train more consistently and I enjoyed every mile of the race, winning in a time almost a minute faster!

As soon as the race ended in 2012, I knew I wanted to run again in 2013. Unfortunately, haphazard training takes a toll and I was injured and out for that year. Then preparing for 2014 I broke my leg (yes, while on a run), was casted for ten weeks, then had to wear a boot before I was cleared to run again in 2014. I went into race day with shaky confidence but my joy to race again, let alone racing the full marathon, overshadowed those nerves. The energy of the event helped carry me to my first win at the Flying Pig Marathon. Something about the Flying Pig weekend ignites my true love of running, racing and community.

Just like the half marathon, winning the full made me want to run again in 2015 to see if I could run it faster and not have any doubts from injuries. I managed to get through the following spring without any major mishaps and I was able to beat my time and cross the finish line, breaking the tape again (as awkward as that is for a short runner).

The very best thing about being part of a Flying Pig event is watching everyone I know line up and crush their goals and do something spectacular. I feel excited and giddy watching the finish line. That adrenaline rush happens all over again. Flying Pig Sunday is the best day of the year for Cincinnati, whether you are a runner in a race, a spectator or a volunteer, because you know the whole city is out rallying for great memories, achieved goals and an overall magical day!

Left: Male marathon winner, Adam Gloyeske.

Right: Female marathon winner, Amy Robillard.

CINCINNATI
ALL★STAR GAME
20 15
JULY 14 • FOX
JULY 14 • FOX
CINCINNATI REDS HALL OF FAME
Joe Nuxhall Way

2716
10079

All Star
GRUNT

Panorama
APARTMENTS
Keep up
the pace,
or I'll hit you with my cane
We got up
early for this,
make us proud
Panorama
Hurry,
this sign is heavy

RUN!
BLACK GIRLS
Run!
FLYING PIG
HALF MARATHON
asics
18443
IGS ENERGY
BLACK GIRLS
Run!
asics
19092

& Loving in Jesus

SHE NEVER GAVE UP.
Lauren Hill 1995 - 2015 #22
NEITHER SHOULD YOU.
CLUB22
THE CURE STARTS NOW
PAIN IS TEMPORARY. PRIDE IS FOREVER
you've come this FAR... finish STRONG!

Buckeye
4697
Buckeye
3117

2263

QUEEN CITY
RUNNING CLUB
5617
MIAMI
5616
895
2930
QUEEN CITY
RUNNING CLUB
5637

Kelly-Carol
Foundation
6529

April 29–May 1, 2016

18th annual Cincinnati Flying Pig Marathon weekend powered by P&G

The Flying Pig added the "Extra Cheese" division to 3-way and 4-way events, including Friday night's Little Kings Mile. Also added were Squadron add-on medals for five, ten and fifteen years of participation.

Running Down a Dream

By Sergio Reyes

Sergio Reyes has singlehandedly re-written the Flying Pig record book with five victories in the marathon, just missing the event record in his first win by a mere 12 seconds.

To say that the Flying Pig Marathon holds a special place for me would be an understatement. The start of 2009 was a return to marathon running for me and little did I know that the marathons I ran that year would fuel the flame for me to race them every year since.

I started the year with my eyes set on Boston and planning went great in terms of training and health. However, as most runners can attest, even if everything in your control goes great, it can be the few remaining things out of your control that can make or break a big day.

That year, it was slight headwinds which made for a harder day. The conditions, compounded with my inexperience of Boston's undulating hills, resulted in me placing 17th in a 2:19. That was just a couple minutes off my goal pace, but a couple minutes too many for my contentment.

Slightly frustrated over all that hard work without a new personal best to show for it, I flew home and thought about where to go from there. My sister, who lived in Cincinnati at the time and was attending my alma mater (Cedarville University), told me it was time for a visit. Call it spontaneous, call it stupidity, but I figured I might as well visit and run Cincinnati's historic event.

A mere thirteen days after Boston, I toed the line looking to just run and have fun with it. What happened next was the body's profound ability to utilize muscle memory and fast recovery in order to engage race pace once again. I didn't even have personal fluids or gels along the way. I simply got out smart, and then started to just run however I felt. I didn't look at the clock and I was unaware of any course record.

I would go on to win that day in a time on par with my Boston performance and close to the course record. However, for me, it was the joy of winning my first marathon ever that gave me the extreme elation I was experiencing.

Over the next seven years, I returned four more times to race the Pig, each one with slightly different goals. Once it was to run faster, once to run after injury recovery, most with the hopes of winning, but *every* time was to put to the test this God-given ability in some manner or another and delight in doing just that. Running with the intent of having fun is what made it enjoyable and go by fast.

It'd also be remiss of me to not highlight the enjoyment of having family, friends, and Flying Pig organizers I'd grown accustomed to seeing, waiting at the finish line for me. The Pig fell on the perfect time of year for me and so I had it annually on my calendar in the hope that things would line up and I could make the trek out, enjoy the city in the Spring, visit the family, catch a Reds game, and ya know, maybe jump in a marathon.

Left: Male marathon winner, Sergio Reyes.

Right: Female marathon winner, Anne Flower.

2016

SUMMER 2016
13075
4176

7961
8015
12178

I HATE
RUNNIN
FLYING PIG HALF MARATHON
11472

RUN
CIN
CIN
NATI
2652

AULT PARK
1587
2916

STOP
POL

2991

Holli Alexander
YOU go girl !!
Here's to your first Marathon! God's Speed (and endurance) be with you! Doyle Rules!!!!
Keep Going
Speckled Stallion!
WE LOVE YOU! (LIKE EVERY CLICHÉ POSTER HERE) NOW FINISH STRONG! JUST DO IT!
Shelley! Happy Birthday! Who's idea was this!!!! Love ya, Myra
Way to go Beth! You can do this! You are amazing and
Steph Kollm-
You can fly to the finish from here!
First time is the best time!!
Way to go Strenker Diane! Next time Boston??

RUN
4569
805
team mitch
6793
6794

FLYING PIG
MARATHON
asics
2991

EDNA
Girl Power
FLYING PIG OPEN RELAY
CINCINNATI
BLACK GIRLS RUN!
FLYING PIG
MARATHON
OPEN RELAY
6726
2016 FLYING PIG OPEN RELAY

Walmart
Sam's Club

1:23:12
5
P&G
7995
1697

May 5–7, 2017

19th annual Cincinnati Flying Pig Marathon weekend powered by P&G

A record number of charities, 340, partnered with the Pig at all levels this year, along with a record of more than 8,000 volunteer spots for the full weekend.

If At First You Don't Succeed...

By Kerry Lee

After coming in second or third in the Flying Pig Marathon for six years, the seventh time proved to be the charm in 2017 for Anderson High School cross country coach Kerry Lee, who won the women's division of the 19th annual Cincinnati Flying Pig Marathon. Lee, who won in a time of 2:53:55, came in second in 2016 as well as in 2015, 2013 and 2011 and was third in the women's field in 2012 and 2014.

The Flying Pig Marathon brings our community together. We have thousands of runners who train to be a part of this very special event every year. It's invigorating on Saturday and Sunday mornings from January to May to see all of those feet hitting the ground on the local routes with local training groups. New friendships are formed, goals are made, lifestyles are improved, lasting memories are created.

Personally, I have been involved in the Flying Pig in some aspect almost every single year since its inception. I've done the 5 Mile, 5K, 10K, 2-person relay, half marathon, Pace Team, and the last seven years in a row I have raced the full marathon. I have loved every single event but the full marathon has the most pull on my heart.

I ran shorter distances competitively for a long time but started running marathons in 2005. As a coach, I always tell my athletes to set multiple goals, so I did that for myself, too. I wanted to qualify for Boston, I wanted to break three hours, and I wanted to someday win the Flying Pig (#1 goal).

I ran many marathons before attempting the Pig to make sure I knew what I was doing. In fact, I ran ten marathons before my first Pig—and then it took me seven of those in a row and twenty-five total marathons to finally win it. Why did I care so much? Because I wanted to win my hometown marathon in front of past, present, and future student athletes of mine. I wanted to show them what it meant to set a goal and go after it—even after failing many, many times. I wanted them to see all of the lessons learned along the way and that hard work does pay off.

One of my favorite parts of the course of the Pig is the Layup for Lauren at Mile 22. (In memory of Lauren Hill, a basketball player at Mt. St. Joseph University who passed away from a brain tumor but inspired the nation to do a "Layup for Lauren" to raise money for brain cancer research.) Many of us use running as an opportunity to express our passion, drive, and dedication to something or someone.

We all have run *for* something or someone and that is truly powerful. In 2017, I ran *for* and *with* my team in the Flying Pig. Throughout that journey, those four boys gave me an incredible amount of dedication, commitment, time, effort, trust and *belief*. Crossing that line with them is something that can never be matched. I will forever remember the 2017 Pig as the year *we* won. ☺

Left: Male marathon winner, Jack Randall.

Right: Female marathon winner, Kerry Lee.

RICK WEBER...
RUNNING THE
P19
YEARS AND
COUNTING
CONGRATULATIONS
RICK WEBER
& DAVE KREKELER

CINCINNATI
RIGHT
TURN
SIGNAL

GO NORTH
CAROLINA
Believe
Be Fearless
&
Fight Back!
SYRACUSE
PIGGIES!
YOUR PIGMOJO
WILL CARRY
YOU 26.2
My Lover is
a Beast
Congrats on
Squadron Level

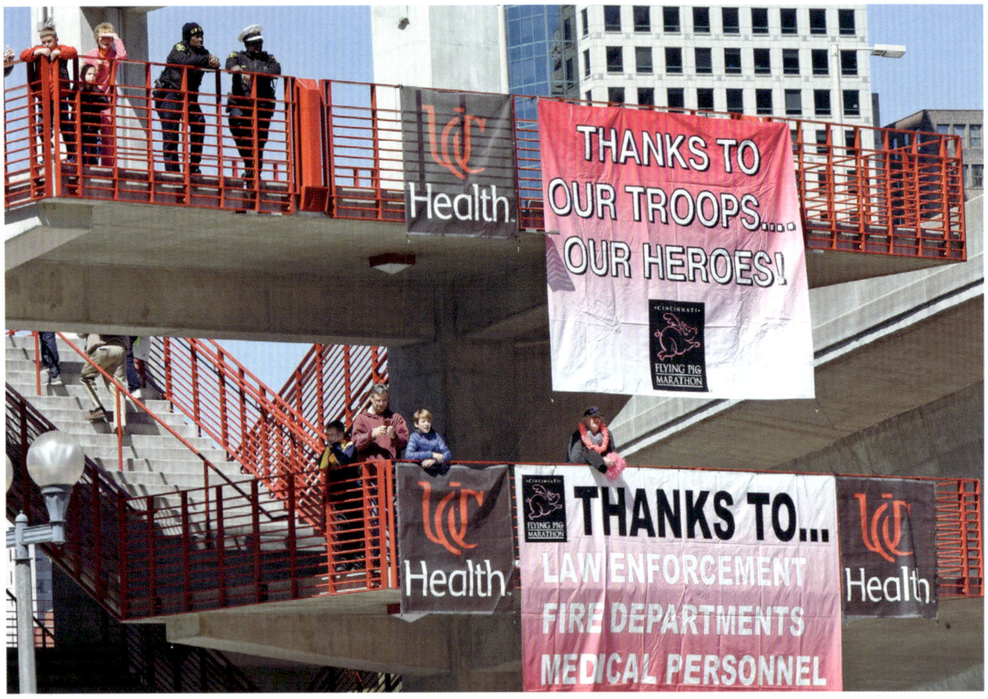
Health
THANKS TO
OUR TROOPS....
OUR HEROES!
FLYING PIG MARATHON
Health
THANKS TO...
LAW ENFORCEMENT
FIRE DEPARTMENTS
MEDICAL PERSONNEL
Health

2017

STREAKER
FLYING PIG MARATHON

FINISH SWINE
ΑΦΑ

FINISH SWINE
asics
tremor
Paycor
Burke
1:02:48
Walmart
FLYING PIG MARATHON

Run
Quest
travel
153

THIS IS NO
TIME TO BE
SOBER
5019

May 4–6, 2018

20th annual Cincinnati Flying Pig Marathon weekend powered by P&G

The 20th anniversary event saw a record 43,127 participants and the debut of the Coughlin Family Cup, with the winners of the marathon receiving an exclusive Rookwood Pottery plaque as their winners' trophy, along with a cash donation to be made to the charity of their choice.

An Anniversary to Remember

By Iris Simpson Bush, Executive Director
Cincinnati Flying Pig Marathon powered by P&G

Iris Simpson Bush has been involved with the Flying Pig almost from day one, from a board member to executive director. Most recently she was named 2017 MarathonFoto/Road Race Management Race Director of the Year and was named to the Running USA Hall of Champions in 2018.

As we celebrated our 20th anniversary of the Flying Pig, many people asked me what our vision was to get to our 20th year. I always say, we were more concerned about just getting the first year under our belts, much less twenty!

When we originally started talking about starting a local marathon, we thought there would be interest among our growing running population in Greater Cincinnati, but just didn't think too far outside our area. We felt our 'hook' to bring people to our event, would be the event itself, starting with the name. A lot of names were put up on the board for debate, including "Seven Hills Marathon" (now that's an enticing name for a runner, isn't it?), "Ohio River Marathon," but when someone put up "Flying Pig Marathon," everyone smiled. And we knew we had a marketing hit on our hands.

Once we had the name, now we had to come up with the event. From the beginning, our goal was to over-deliver on everything–more water stops, more premium gifts (not ala carte, but included with registration), more entertainment, more "street squealers" to cheer on the participants. And from day one, we wanted charities to use our event to raise money for their own groups. As a 501 c3, the Flying Pig Marathon uses its non-profit status as a conduit for charities and their own fundraising–more than $16 million so far.

In the early years we depended on so many great people to get us going, including our first executive director Mike Boylan, our first race director, the late Rich Williams, then later executive directors including Kelly Weissmann, who also worked with Don Connolly on managing our race events, and Scott Maier, who had been with the board since its inception. They built the foundation, along with people and organizations who believed in our mission and were there to support us, like P&G, Asics, Tremor and Paycor, without whom we could not have gotten the Flying Pig off the ground. And our medical team and first responders are vital to keeping our participants safe.

Personally, there are so many people I would like to thank, starting with my husband, Jim, whom I met on the Flying Pig board, and my family who still answers my calls when I need volunteers to work an event. Our Flying Pig board continues to have the vision and the drive to keep this event growing, and our stellar Flying Pig staff is the best any race event could have.

As for the next twenty years, I feel that our founders have given us the structure to sustain the Flying Pig for many years to come, but it is up to us to listen to what our participants want. More than ten years ago they asked for a separate half marathon event, and now it's the largest event we have. They asked for a multi-event challenge, so we came up with the Skyline Chili 3-Way and 4-Way (*and* extra cheese). What will they want next? Whatever the 'next' is, I'm confident our board and our staff will be able to handle it.

It's been an amazing twenty years. I've been fortunate to see this event soar to new heights, and I'm looking forward to many more years of spreading my wings with our Flying Pigs.

Flying Pig Board of Directors, front row, L-R: Doug Olberding, Ed.D.; Frances Gilbert; Bob Coley; Barbara Walker, Ph.D.; Dr. Jon Divine; John Sence; Bob Coughlin. *Back row, L-R:* Dr. Thomas Kimball; Bob Baron; Michael Laux; James Jansing; Dr. Holly Ippisch; James Ferguson; Mike Boylan; Jon Roketenetz; Josh Heuser; Katy Bunn; Bob Roncker; Jeff Kujawa; Jim Mahon.

FLYING PIG MARATHON BOARD OF TRUSTEES

2018 FLYING PIG STREAKERS

(those who completed the first nineteen Flying Pig Marathons)

William Abplanalp
Charles Altenau
Myles Apo
Don Belfort
Jennifer Black
Jay Brewer
John Buch
Howard Buchanan
Daniel Canter
Ken Chestek
Tim Clement
Alan Coppinger
J Jill Cummins
Tim Cuttle
Jim Devanney
Gregory Doench
Mick Dollenmayer
Steve Dressing
John Ebel
Bleda Elibal
Bob Engel
Kevin Eustace
Rosemary Evans
Ed Ferrell
Ron Foster
Paul Franke
Mark A. Freeman
Kathleen Fussinger
Jack Gray
Bill Haber
Shelly Haber
Keith Hall
Michael Hauser
Kevin Hensley
Wayne Hinaman
Jeffrey Hirsch
Martin Hovey
Paul Hudak
Mark Jepson
John Keegan
Rick Kieser
Mark Koors
David Krekeler
Harvey Lewis
Mike Lies
Rick Lukin
Michael Marrero
Billie Jo Mendoza
Scott Momburg
Michael Oeder
James Patterson
Glen Paulsen
Steve Pfeffer
Toby Pinger
Mark Pruden
Perry Ralenkotter
Michael Rath
Diane Rose
Ronald Ross
Scott Rudy
Mark Sackett
Kathy Schickel
Amy Schmidt
Jean Schmidt
Kenneth Sirois
Phyllis Sizemore
Lonnie Smith
Mike Smith
Kenneth Sova
Rod Spearman
Rob Sprengard
Steve Strickler*
Keith Tenoever
Steve Torok
Jim Venters
Jim Walsh
Arden Wander
Cary Watson
Rick Weber
Mark Wehry
Michael Weisgerber
Ron Weitzenkorn
James Welland
Richard White
Brian K. Young
David Krekeler
Stephan Young
Nancy Zadek

**In Memoriam. His bib was carried along the 2018 course and is now retired.*

TOYOTA 20 DAYS ON THE RUN IN PARTNERSHIP WITH QUEEN CITY RUNNING

To celebrate the 20th anniversary of the Cincinnati Flying Pig Marathon powered by P&G, the marathon scheduled twenty days of community activities leading up to Flying Pig weekend. From a celebrity torch run kickoff to beer runs, yoga, baseball and marathon route cleanup, the Flying Pig said "thanks" for twenty years of being part of the Greater Cincinnati community!

2018

FLYING PIG
MARATHON
PRE-ORDER YOUR 20TH
ANNIVERSARY
FLYING PIG MARATHON
BOOK TODAY!
VISIT WWW.FLYINGPIGMARATHON.COM
TO PRE-ORDER FOR $29.95
THANKS TO

THE PIGGYs PRESENTED BY P&G

As part of the 20th anniversary, the Flying Pig Marathon held the inaugural PIGGYs awards presented by P&G at the Aronoff Center for the Performing Arts on Thursday, May 3, to pay tribute to those who have made the race successful over the last twenty years. More than 1,000 people attended the PIGGYs, which honored Boston Marathon race director Dave McGillivray, the eighty-six Streakers who had completed the nineten previous marathons, first responders, charities and long-time supporters of the Flying Pig.

2018

CINCINNATI
WLWT

CINCINNATI
FLYING PIG
MARATHON

THE PIGGYS

KEEPSAKES, FLYING PIG MURAL MARK 20TH ANNIVERSARY

The Flying Pig's 20th anniversary celebration began in October of 2017 with the dedication of the downtown "Dream Big and Fly High" mural, created by ArtWorks and made possible by the Coughlin Family Foundation. At the P&G Health & Fitness Expo, Rookwood Pottery commemoratives and The Verdin Company anniversary bell were part of the participants' expo experience.

FLYING PIG PARTIES

Friday evening's VIP party expanded into the downtown streets where, after the Piggest Raffle Ever Drop presented by Stock Yards Bank, a free concert headlined by DJ ETrayn, Moonbeau, Telehope and Coin entertained the crowd and kicked off Flying Pig weekend.

LITTLE KINGS MILE

The second leg of the TQL Beer Series, the Little Kings Mile, kicked off the Friday evening schedule. Winning in the men's elite division was Jacob Edwards of Delaware, Ohio, who won the event in 2016, second was Alex Beruscha of Louisville and third was Zach Beavin of Lexington, Kentucky. In the women's elite division, Flannery Musk from Louisville was the first finisher, with Emma McCarron of Mansfield, Ohio, second and Lara Crofford, the Little Kings Mile winner in 2016 and Paycor Half Marathon winner in 2017, coming in third.

Little Kings Mile elite women, L-R: Flannery Musk, first; Emma McCarron, second; Lara Crofford, third.

Little Kings Mile elite men, L-R: Jacob Edwards, first; Alex Beruscha, second, Zach Beavin, third.

SATURDAY AT THE FLYING PIG

From the Toyota 10K to the mascot race, Flying Piglet, Flying Fur and PigAbilities, Saturday's events had something for everyone with more than 17,000 participating.

Toyota 10K top three, L-R: Marco Pettenazzo, third; Chris Reischel, first; Luke Ogden, second.

Toyota 10K female division top three, L-R: Lauren Carnahan, third; Lucia Rodbro, first; Laura Bill, second with Flying Pig executive director Iris Simpson Bush.

Tri-State Running Company 5K top three, L-R: Ethan Weaver, third; Benjamin Spratt, first; Brian Drapp, second.

Tri-State Running Company 5K female division top three, L-R: Marie Wysong, third; Alison Delgado, first, Rita Mayer, second.

TEAM

PIGLET · DIAPER DASH
Pampers
START LINE
FIRST WATCH
42864

PIGLET · DIAPER DASH
Pampers
START LINE
FIRST WATCH
CINCINNATI

DADDY
ULTRA

Sprint

2018

asics
Burke
CityDash
Paycor
FINISH SWINE

GOODWILL
PIGABILITIES
48521

48502
48543

FINISH SWINE

49328

48830
49184

6817

TEAM
Flying Pig
CINCINNATI FLYING PIG MARATHON

Kroger

7 HILLS RUN
20375

START LINE

adidas
17209

ST. MARGARET HALL
Skilled Nursing Assisted Living

YOU THINK YOU'RE TIRED...
TRY HOLDING THIS SIGN FOR 15 MINUTE
I Like Pig Butts and I Cannot Lie.
Toenails are for losers!

5430

Paycor
P&G

P&G
asics
Kroger
Paycor

RECORD FIELD FOR 20TH ANNIVERSARY

The 20th running of the Flying Pig Marathon powered by P&G crowned two first-time Pig winners, Aaron Viets, 28, of Cedarburg, WI, and former Cincinnatian Caitlin Keen, 25, now living in Fort Worth.

For their wins, the Coughlin Family Foundation provided a Rookwood Pottery tile to Viets and Keen, along with a $2,500 donation to be made to the charity of their choice. Viets' donation went to Lutherans for Life and Keen's check went to her former elementary school, St. Mary's in Hyde Park.

Flying Pig participants were able to parade on the field with their medals at the Cincinnati Reds game the next evening at the annual "Pig Night at the Ball Park" as Caitlin threw out the first pitch.

Caitlin Keen gets ready to throw out the first pitch at the Cincinnati Reds game May 7.

Men's marathon winner Aaron Viets talks to reporters.

Women's marathon winner Caitlin Keen greets her mom, Kim, at the finish.

Paycor Half Marathon top 3: Andrew Bryan, 3rd; winner Jack Butler; Zack Beavin, 2nd.

Paycor Half Marathon top 3: Daniella Orton, 3rd; Molly Trachtenberg, winner; Katie Lenahan, 2nd with executive director Iris Simpson Bush.

Paycor Half Marathon wheelchair winner: Marc vanRafelghem with Iris Simpson Bush.

Iris Simpson Bush, Micah Carroll, CEO, The Rookwood Pottery Company, Aaron Viets, Caitlin Keen and Flying Pig founder Bob Coughlin present the winners with their Coughlin Family Cup Rookwood tiles.

Flying Pig participants parade on the field on Pig Night at the Ball Park May 7.

2018
2018
2018
FINISHER
22401
22126

FINISH SWINE

2018 CINCINNATI FLYING PIG MARATHON
20 YEARS RUNNING

OUR SPONSORS

PRESENTING SPONSORS

Powered by P&G · asics · Kroger · Paycor · tremor

PLATINUM SPONSORS

All Whites · Burke · Cincinnati Bell connecting what matters · CityDash Your Delivery Solution · GEICO · Skyline Chili · UC Health · WLWT5 · Zumbiel Packaging

GOLD SPONSORS

Buckeye · Cincinnati Business Courier · DHL · EY Building a better working world · First Student Charter Bus Rental · First Watch The Daytime Cafe · Fleet Feet Sports · GigSmart · JackRabbit · LaRosa's Family Pizzeria · Michelob Ultra · Pampers · Sprint · Toyota Let's Go Places · Tri-State Running Company

SILVER SPONSORS

Art's Rental Equipment & Supply · Barefoot · Caruso · Cincinnati USA.com · Cincinnati · CVG Cincinnati/Northern Kentucky International Airport · Dick's Sporting Goods · Dole · Executive Transportation · G Endurance · Goodwill we put people to work! · Health Carousel · iHeartMedia Cincinnati · KMK Law · Melink Energy solutions for a brighter tomorrow · Mount St. Joseph University · Pure Protein · RoadID It's Who I Am · Rookwood Pottery Company · Rumpke · Stock Yards Bank & Trust Since 1904 · 3 Sweet Girls Cakery · TQL · Two Men and a Truck "Movers Who Care." · Ultimate Air Shuttle

BRONZE SPONSORS

always · Bounty · Cascade · Charmin · Crest · Dawn · Downy · Gain · head & shoulders · Ivory · Olay · Old Spice · Oral-B · Pampers · Safeguard · Secret · Tampax · Tide · attendance on demand · BDG Bell Dental Group · Boogie Wipes · Buffalo Wings & Rings · Cintas Ready for the Workday · Invisible Fence Brand · Kroger · New Life Furniture Bank · Pepsi-Cola · Pete DeLois recreations · Pure Romance · Sunbelt Bakery · U.S. Army · Greater Cincinnati Water Works

THANKS TO...

The Alleen Co. Rentals, Inc. · Ampac · Barefoot Proximity · Brand Evolutions · The City of Cincinnati · The City of Cincinnati Office of Environment & Sustainability · The City of Covington · The City of Newport · Game Day Communications · Hamilton County · Hamilton County Recycling and Solid Waste District · Keep Cincinnati Beautiful · Nutrition Council · Public Library of Cincinnati · Road Runners Club of America · SCS Engineering · Season's 52 · Southbank Partners · Spectra · Trophy Awards · Village of Fairfax · Village of Mariemont · Xavier University

SPECIAL THANKS TO THOSE WHO KEEP US SAFE...

Our Police and Fire Department in Cincinnati, Covington, Fairfax, Hamilton County, Mariemont and Newport; Department of Homeland Security, FBI and the Flying Pig Marathon Medical Team.

20th ANNIVERSARY SPONSORS

Powered by P&G · asics · CE Power · The Carol Ann and Ralph V. Haile, Jr. US Bank Foundation · Fleet Feet Sports · Paycor · Palomino Restaurant & Bar · Rookwood Pottery Company · Queen City Running · The Project 100.7 106.3 · Toyota Let's Go Places

The sponsors listed above made their commitment to the Flying Pig Marathon prior to the deadline for the production of these bags.

2018 FLYING PIG CHARITY PARTNERS

The Flying Pig Marathon Charity Program provides four (4) avenues for charities to utilize the Flying Pig events (5K, 10K, Flying Fur, Open Relay, Half-marathon, Full Marathon, 3-Way, 3-Way with Cheese, 4-Way & 4-Way with Cheese) as a fundraiser. Over the last twenty years, the Flying "Piganthropy" program has helped participating charities to collectively raise more than $16 million.

PARTNER CHARITIES

Adopt A Class
ALSAC/St. Jude's Children's Research Hospital
Alzheimer's Association of Greater Cincinnati
Autism Society of Greater Cincinnati
Back 2 Back Ministries
CancerFree Kids
Children's Dyslexia Centers of Cincinnati–Wee Boys Runners
City Gospel Mission
Cradle Cincinnati Supporting Black Girls Run!
Cystic Fibrosis Foundation
debra of America
DKMS: We Delete Blood Cancer
Dress for Success Cincinnati
Fragile X Family Alliance
Freedom 4/24
Girls on the Run Greater Cincinnati
Haunnah Meyer Memorial Fund
`Honor Run Foundation
Intercommunity Justice & Peace Center
International Myeloma Foundation
JDRF Southwest Ohio
Joel Cornette Foundation
Lauren's Fight for Cure
Living Arrangements for the Developmentally Disabled
Make-A-Wish Ohio, Kentucky & Indiana
Mayfield Education & Research Foundation
McAuley High School
Melanoma Know More
Miles That Matter Foundation
Move for Hunger
Muscular Dystrophy Association of Southern Ohio
National Down Syndrome Society
Ohio Valley Voices
Parent Project Muscular Dystrophy
Run for the Call
Servant's Heart Haiti Mission
Shriners Hospital for Children-Cincinnati
SPCA Cincinnati
Team Grace
The Children's Home of Cincinnati
The Leukemia & Lymphoma Society's Team in Training
Whole Again
Wood Hudson Cancer Research Laboratory, Inc.

ASSOCIATE CHARITIES

Adopt A Class
Adore-A-Bull Rescue
American Council of the Blind of Ohio, Greater Cincinnati Chapter
Cancer Family Care
Catholics United for the Poor
Celebrating Restoration
Center for Addiction Treatment
Circle Tail, Inc.
Cris Collinsworth ProScan Fund
Junior Achievement of OKI Partners, Inc.
Lighthouse Youth & Family Services
LuMind RDS
Ronald McDonald House Charities of Greater Cincinnati
Run for the Future Scholarship (West Clermont Education Foundation)
Special Olympics Hamilton County
Summit Academy Community School for Alternative Learners-Middletown
The Dragonfly Foundation
WordPlay Cincy
World Child Cancer USA

VOLUNTEER CHARITIES

Alembic Lodge No. 793 F.&A.M
American Cancer Society-Pan Ohio Hope Ride
American Council of the Blind of Ohio
Anderson Expos
Anderson High School Band
Anderson High school Boys Lacrosse
Anderson High School Football
Anderson High School Girls Lacrosse
Anderson Hills UMC
Arthritis Foundation
Arthritis Walk - Team McElfresh
Athletes In Action
Avondale Running Club
Bec's Bunch
Beckfield College Association of Nursing Students
Bike Team
Boy Scout Troop 107
Boy Scout Troop 155
Boy Scout Troop 170
Boy Scout Troop 468
Boy Scout Troop 519
Boy Scout Troop 617
Boy Scout Troop 727
Boy Scout Venture Crew 522
Boys Hope Girls Hope
Brighton Center
Buffalo Wings & Rings
Burke Fan Zone
Carl Linder YMCA
CBTS Volunteers
Center for Addiction Treatment
Center for Independent Living Options (CILO)
CHICO Memorial Scholarship Fund
Childrens Home of Cincinnati
Christ Emmanual Church
Cin-City Gators - Friday
Cin-City Gators - Sunday
Cincinnati Broomball Association
Cincinnati Cardinals
Cincinnati Elite Double Dutch Team
Cincinnati Icebreakers Sled Hockey
Cincinnati Museum Center
Cincinnati Parrothead Club
Cincinnati Pit Crew
Cincinnati Rotary Club
Cincy Doom - Taylor
Cincy Royal Crush
Cincy Slammers Black '04
Cincy Slammers Fastpitch - Ripperger
Cincy Slammers- Jones
Cincy Slammers-Hartzler
Cincy Slammers-Sweeney
CircleTail
Clark Montessori Girls Basketball
Clinton-Massie Softball
Colerain Young Life
Communities United for Action
Cooper Girls Basketball
Covington Latin
Crossroads Church
Delta Eta Eta, Chi Eta Phi
Delta Kappa Gamma
Delta Sigma Theta
Devicor Medical Products
DHL for Cancer Free Kids
Diamond Oaks SkillsUSA
Diocesan Catholic Children's home
Down to Earth 4-H Club
Dramakinetics
East End Area Council
EC Trojan Football Boosters
EY
Fairfax Group
Finish Line Pros
Finneytown Falcons Youth Association
First Missionary Baptist Church
Flex Fund Boosters
Forest Hills Special Education Program
Fragile X Family Alliance
Friends of Harriet Beecher Stowe House
GE Volunteers for LLS
Girl Scout Troop 41051
Girlfriends Giving Back
Goshen High School
Grace to Africa
Gray Middle School
Great Oaks
Greater Cincinnati Choral Union Inc
Green Team Sunday
Greyhound Adoption of Greater Cincinnati
Guardian Angels Boy Scout Troop 445
Guiding Light Mentoring
Haunnah Meyer Memorial Fund
Highlands Band Association - Expo
HOSA
House of Run N Tri
Insurance Professionals of Greater Cincinnati
Ishtar #54 Daughters of the Nile
It's Working Out
Kelly Carol Foundation
Kemba Credit Union
Kindervelt #16 of Children's Hospital
Kindervelt #57
Ladies of Glamour
Lakota East HS Student Government
Lakota West Cross Country Team
LaSalle High School Hockey Team
LaSalle Highschool Drama
Lauren's Fight for Cure
Les Birdies Golf Club
Leukemia & Lymphoma Society - Light the Night Walk
Leukemia Lymphoma Society
Lincoln Heights Missionary Baptist Boy Scout 772
Little Miami Softball
Live Oaks SkillsUSA
Lucky Tales Rescue
Madisonville Citizens on Patrol
Madisonville Education & assistance Center
Majestic Generation Christian Dance Team
Mariemont Community Church
Marjorie Book Continuing Education
Mark Reckman Scholarship
McAuley High School
McNicholas High School Band
McNicholas High School Dance Team
McNicholas High School Football
McNicholas Men's Volleyball
McNicholas Women's Basketball
McNicholas Women's Soccer
Melink
Midwest Takeover Basketball
Milford Band Boosters
Milford Highschool Cross Country
Milford Kiwanis Club
Moeller Highschool Band
Mommy Has Breast Cancer
Montezuma-Cincinnati Detachment 270 - Marine Corps
Mt Washington Presbyterian Church Troop 112
Muscular Dystrophy Association of Southern Ohio
My Nose Turns Red
National Federation of the Blind of Ohio
Nativity Athletic Boosters
Never the Less
New City Presbyterian Church
New Richmond High School Marching Band
Newport Central Catholic
NKY Bandits
Noize - 90 - 0774569
Northstar Girl Scouts
Northwest Younglife
Norwood Cheerleaders
Oak Hills UMC Women
Ohio Valley Chapter of the Hutchinson Bell
Ohio Valley Scottish Society
Paddling for Cancer Awareness
Paws & Claws Animal Rescue
Pay it Forward Cincinnati
Paycor
Paycor - Finish Line
People for DD Services
Pi Kappa Phi Fraternity - Theta Chapter
Pool Foundation
Princeton High School Softball
Project 4His Glory - Sunday Group
Purcell Marian High School
Queen City Emergency Net
Reading Band Boosters
Runner's Club of Cincinnati
Saint Ursula Track & Field
Scarlet Oaks
School for the Creative and Performing Arts
Scott High School
Scott High School Junior Statesmen of America
Sidekicks Made
Sigma Gamma Rho
Sigma Theta Tau
SPCA
St. Andrews Episcopal Church
St. Barbara Youth Group
St. Henry Highschool
St. Joseph Consolidated School
St. Mark Missionary Baptist Church
STAF - Save The Animals Foundation
Strategic Franchising
Sycamore High School Hockey Team
Taylor High School Soccer
Team OHC for LLS
Ten Fe
The Healthcare Connection
TLC Barefoot School
Tom Geiger Guest House
Tri-State Bleeding Disorder Foundation
Tri-State Volunteers
Trinity Episcopal Church
Turpin Highschool Boys Track Team
Turpin Highschool Girls Track Team
UC - Kappa Kappa Gamma
UC - Sigma Chi
UC Mountaineering
UC Waterski
Ulster Project
US Air Force 338th Recruiting Squadron
Valley Temple Sisterhood
Venture Crew 805
Villa Madonna Academy
Walnut Hills Cheerleaders
Walnut Hills Green Team
Walnut Hills High School Cross Country
Walnut Hills Highschool Touchdown Club
Wesley Chapel Mission
Wesley Community Services
West Clermont Cross Country
West Clermont Dive - Vintage
West Clermont High School Band Boosters
West Clermont High School Cheerleading
West Clermont High School Football
Western Hills Athletic Association
Western Hills HS Football
Western Hills HS Key Club
Westwood First Presbyterian Church Women
Whole Again
Wilmington College Sports Club
Worldpay
Wright-Patterson Air Force Base Top III
Wyoming Citizens Police Academy Alumni Assoc
Young Life Princeton High School
Young Marines of Cincinnati
Zion Lutheran Church

PIGGEST RAFFLE CHARITIES

Adopt A Book
Adopt a Class
Alzheimer's Association of Greater Cincinnati
American Council of the Blind of Ohio, Greater Cincinnati Chapter
Angel's Rest Animal Sanctuary
Animal Friends Humane Society
Archbishop McNicholas Band Boosters
Autism Society Greater Cincinnati
Beech Acres Parenting Center
Big Brothers Big Sisters of Greater Cincinnati
Bluegrass Pug Rescue, Inc.
Brighton Recovery Center
Cancer Family Care
CASA for Clermont Kids
Cat Adoption Team
Catholics United for the Poor
Celebrating Restoration
Center for Addiction Treatment
Center for Independent Living Options, Inc.
Children's Dyslexia Centers of Cincinnati - Wee Boys Runners
Cincinnati Therapeutic Riding & Horsemanship
Circle Tail, Inc.
City Gospel Mission
Communities United For Action
Fernside: A Center for Grieving Children
Fourgotten Paws Animal Rescue
Franciscan Ministries, Inc.
Friends of Tiny Hearts
Girls on the Run Cincinnati
Greater Cincinnati World Affairs Council
Harlequin Haven Great Dane Rescue
HART - Homeless Animal Rescue Team of Cincinnati
Haunnah Meyer Memorial Fund
JDRF Southwest Ohio
Journey to Hope
Lauren's Fight for Cure
Living Arrangements for the Developmentally Disabled
Mark Reckman Scholarship
Miles That Matter Foundation
Milford Cross Country
Milford Kiwanis Club
My Nose Turns Red Theatre Co.
National Federation of the Blind of Ohio
New Life Furniture Bank
Ohio Alleycat Resource (OAR)
PawPrints Animal Rescue, Inc.
Recovery Center of Hamilton County
Runners' Club of Greater Cincinnati
Save Our Shelter Dogs
Scleroderma Foundation Ohio Chapter
Servant's Heart Haiti Mission
Snack in Sak
Society of Women Engineers, UC Section
Sojourner Recovery Services
Special Olympics Hamilton County
St. Bernadette School
St. Francis Seraph School
St. Joseph Consolidated School
St. Rita School for the Deaf
Stayin' Alive, Inc.
Susan G. Komen Southwest Ohio
Team RWB
The Children's Home of Cincinnati
The Dragonfly Foundation
The Leukemia and Lymphoma Society
Valley Interfaith Community Resource Center
Wesley Chapel Mission Center
Wood Hudson Cancer Research Laboratory, Inc.

A Final Word...

By Joe Hale

Joe Hale was there for the beginning of the Flying Pig Marathon, serving on the board while serving as VP and chief communications officer of Cinergy Corp. (now Duke Energy) and as president of the Cinergy Foundation. He ran seven marathons on seven continents in seven months in 2005 and raised $190,000 for the March of Dimes. In 2016 he was named executive director of The Nantucket Dreamland, a nonprofit film and performing arts center.

Over twenty years ago, when my friend Bob Coughlin approached me with the idea of starting a marathon in Cincinnati, I jumped at the chance to help. For someone who loved running, community involvement, and Cincinnati, it was a perfect confluence of my interests.

As our board was recruited and ideas turned to reality, I was fortunate to play a variety of roles in the Flying Pig Marathon, from volunteer fundraiser to board chair, from runner (my good friend Bill Keating, Jr. always loved to remind me of the year he insisted I stop mid-course so he could take my photo and I finished in 4 hours and 5 seconds, just over my goal of breaking 4 hours that year because of his photo op!) to finish line chair, where I got to personally congratulate/hug each sweaty finisher of our race.

Talk about inspiring!

I am so very proud of the race today—ranked among the country's finest and best organized—thanks to a continued stream of wonderful community volunteers. Our marathon has always been known for its "well planned spontaneity," where you never know what to expect around the next corner—from a 50-voice choir singing "You Lift Me Up" with a backdrop of the sun rising over the Ohio River, to the child with a hand-lettered sign that simply says "I'm proud of you" that comes just when a runner needs that little boost of encouragement.

Being involved in the Flying Pig Marathon has been a highlight of my running career, a career that has literally taken me around the world. But there's no place like our home town marathon. Thank you for allowing me to play a small part in its creation and growth.

Photographers

THANKS TO OUR FLYING PIG PHOTOGRAPHERS

Over the years, the photographers and videographers at the Flying Pig events and on the course have brought us spectacular images that have made us laugh, cry and celebrate the Flying Pig Marathon. We want to thank those photographers whose contributions have meant so much to this twenty-year celebration.

Michael E. Anderson has been an official Flying Pig photographer since 2003. He rides his mountain bike along the entire course capturing photos and videos of race participants, spectators, volunteers, water stops and entertainment zones from a "runners point of view." Michael is the Public Relations Manager for the Cincinnati Reds and lives in Anderson Township with his wife Melissa and daughters Ella and Molly.

Mark Bowen is a professional free-lance visual content provider who works with Greater Cincinnati's business community. Mark has photographed all but one of the Flying Pig Marathons.

Scott Bowers serves as Executive Director and President of FOCAS Ministries in Cincinnati. His passion for photography was reignited after a mission's trip to Haiti with FOCAS in the summer of 1999. He has been photographing the Flying Pig Marathon since 2006.

Paula Norton has been in the business of photography since 1972 capturing some of the finest visual images of Cincinnati USA and its business/civic leaders through her corporate portrait, editorial, events and on-location photography.

Madison Schmidt picked up her first camera in 2009 and immediately began to pursue photography at her high school and college newspapers. During her first Pig, she explored the course shooting for the *Cincinnati Enquirer* in 2016 and one year later started working with Game Day Communications to shoot photo and video with the Flying Pig Marathon.

Jim Talkington has been an advertising and editorial photographer and filmmaker in Cincinnati for more than twenty years. He especially enjoys helping cause-driven organizations and businesses tell their visual stories with honesty and authenticity.

Tom Uhlman has been a free-lance photographer for more than twenty years. He enjoys photographing everything from mother bats in a Texas cave to kids and pets in backyards, as well as CEOs in creative office settings. His art is motivated by the rewards of capturing both scenes of action and the personalities of people he photographs.

Also thanks to: Curt Austin, Sam Bolden, Keith Bowers, Samantha Grier, Ricardo Lemos, and Paul Levy.

Acknowledgments

Flying Pig staff, front row, L-R: John Cappella, Co-Race Director; Sarah Pelfrey, Sales & Marketing Director; Denise Hovey, Director of Sustainability; Iris Simpson Bush, Executive Director; Nikki Broughton, Project Manager; Mary Enzweiler, Course Experience Coordinator. *Back Row, L-R:* Joel Barnhill, Director of Post-Race Events and Charity Coordinator; Jenna Siegrist, Sales & Promotions Manager; John Vesprani, Director of Operations-Signage and Displays; Jeanette Kiley, Volunteer Coordinator; Taylor Conklin, Youth Programs Coordinator; Jen Graham, Accountant/Registration Director. *not pictured: Shawn Verhoff, Co-Race Director.

The staff of the Flying Pig Marathon would like to thank the Carol Ann and Ralph V. Haile Jr. Foundation and its president, Tim Maloney, for funding this 20th anniversary book. We are proud to be included in the many projects and events that the Foundation supports in our community.

We would also like to thank the sponsors who have been with us since day one of the Flying Pig, including P&G, Paycor, Asics and Tremor. You took a chance on this little community event and helped us grow to a $15 million economic impact weekend.

While members of the Flying Pig Board of Directors have changed throughout the years, the mission has not: To put on a world-class event, to celebrate our communities and to raise money for charities. We thank every board member who has served throughout the years.

Speaking of our communities, we would not have been successful over the years without the support of the municipalities the marathon runs through, including the cities of Cincinnati, Covington and Newport, as well as the neighborhoods and townships who let us use their streets, their facilities and their safety personnel. A special "squeal" to our "Street Squealers" who come out every year to cheer the participants on!

For every venue we used for our "Twenty Days on the Run" in partnership with Toyota and Queen City Running, thanks for letting us promote the Flying Pig's anniversary and a special thanks to Todd Duesing and the staff of the Aronoff Center for being gracious hosts for "The PIGGYs." Also, thanks to Prestige Audio Visual and WLWT-TV for making "The PIGGYs" broadcast happen.

Included in our thanks are the Cincinnati Reds for again being the hosts for "Pig Night at the Ball Park" and allowing our finishers to parade around the field. It's always a special night for them.

We know there are hundreds more who have helped make this event possible, and even though you may not be listed, please know that we are grateful for your support. And, finally, thanks to the participants who have made this event one of the top running festivals in the country. We are humbled and inspired by your accomplishments, and your loyalty to our Flying Pig!

In Memoriam

Thousands of volunteers make the Flying Pig run each year. We want to remember three of those who worked tirelessly to launch the Flying Pig two decades ago. Although they are no longer with us, their contributions will never be forgotten.

Al Salvato, a longtime Flying Pig volunteer who also started the New Year's Day Frostbite Run in Northern Kentucky.

John Schmidt Jr., the 2002 chair of the Board of Directors of the Flying Pig.

Rich Williams, the first race director of the Flying Pig Marathon.

FINISH
CINCINNATI
FLYING PIG MARATHON
P&G
MKTG
paycor
3:53·13